In The Quiet of This Place

In The Quiet of This Place

Memorials from the Protestant Chapel
in Tadoussac, Quebec

CASPER PRESS

Published in the United States by Casper Press, Boca Grande, FL

Library of Congress Control Number: 2023906141

ISBN 978-0-9973203-5-0
BISAC 1. BIOGRAPHY/AUTOBIOGRAPHY/General 2. HISTORY/Canada/
Provincial, Territorial & Local/Quebec (QC) 3. HISTORY/Canada /General

Contributing Editors
Michael Alexander, Susie Bruemmer, Alan Evans

Foreword
Alan Evans

Photography credits
Interior of the Protestant Chapel *(front cover)* by Peter Turcot
Exterior of the Protestant Chapel *(back cover)* by Sarah Wallace

Book Cover and Layout
Sally Stetson Design

Learn more about Tadoussac and its history, community,
architecture and wildlife at *tidesoftadoussac.com*

2 4 6 8 10 9 7 5 3 1

*For those people whose stories are in this book,
who gave of themselves to build the
Tadoussac community that we share today.*

Contents

Foreward

Tadoussac has a rich history of indigenous peoples, French and English settlers, and people who call this village home today. As we sit in the quiet of the Tadoussac Protestant Chapel it is easy to feel that sense of history.

Beginning in 1882, the English-speaking community, placed memorials in the chapel. The oldest memorial is of the youngest person – five-month-old Jessie Whitely – memorialized in the windows over the altar. Perhaps her contribution was to start a tradition that now numbers over a hundred memorials in the main church alone. Many of these are for people we remember. Some are from long before our time. Though the names and dates of many may mean little to us today, these memorials are for people with whom we have things in common, including: a love for this area; an appreciation for its beauty; a desire for an enjoyable summer holiday; and perhaps even a willingness to make sacrifices to ensure that their descendants would have this place to retreat to from lives lived elsewhere. They, too, sat where we sit on Sunday mornings taking time out of their holiday activity to reflect upon the big questions of faith.

This book is a collection of stories and biographies of people who are memorialized in the church, specifically within the main body, or nave of the church. They are the oldest, and in some cases, they tell us about the people we know the least about.

In the year 2000, the congregation decided that to preserve the lovely board and batten panelling we should stop placing plaques on the walls of the church. At that time, we began placing much smaller, uniform memorial plaques in the narthex area. We created a binder containing brief biographies for the newer memorials. This book does not include those biographies.

Tadoussac is fortunate to have been visited by some fascinating people who have lived extraordinary lives all over the world. The book tells of the contributions many made to community, their families, friends, and to the country in which they lived. It also tells of those who sacrificed their lives in times of war to help provide the freedom that we enjoy. The Chapel community has wanted their lives to be remembered, so this is a compilation of their stories, mostly written by their descendants.

We are all very thankful to those who have contributed to this book. It would not have been possible without the generous gift of time and energy devoted to gathering past stories and sharing them with family to get additional information.

This memorial book is about the people who have gone before us, many of whom lived in our cottages and bequeathed to us an abiding love of this remarkable place.

Alan Evans
May 2023

The Tadoussac Protestant Chapel –
A Brief History

With the construction of the original Tadoussac Hotel in 1864, tourists and summer residents came to Tadoussac from the surrounding provinces and the United States. Many were English-speaking and represented different Protestant denominations of the Christian church. On Sunday, August 14th, 1864, in his diary, Godfrey Rhodes recorded that: "We always have church under the trees (in front of the hotel.)" [1]

In the late 1800s, the so-called "Indian Chapel" of Ste Croix (1747) was already over a hundred years old. A second church on the road to Moulin Baude also served the Roman Catholic residents. The newer, larger Ste Croix wasn't built until 1884.

On August 21st of 1866, a group of twelve men met in the hotel to commit to the construction of a Protestant chapel to be open only in the summer months. They decided it should be non-denominational because there were a number of different denominations of the Christian church represented in the group of trustees and among the summer residents.

While it is unknown who the architect was, the style is "Carpenter Gothic", the wooden version of "Gothic Revival", common in Canada at the time. "Elements of the style are manifest in the chapel's steeply pitched roof, vertical board and batten siding, in its pointed arched entry, windows, and roof structure, as well as in the forms and details of its interior millwork which are particularly elaborate in the chancel." [2]

When the church was built there were several services each Sunday from the Anglican, Presbyterian, and other traditions, but as time passed the number of Anglicans and as many as five more or less home-grown Anglican clergy pulled the chapel in its own direction. Sometime in the 1900s, the chapel even bought a full set of pew copies of the Anglican

[1] Rhodes, Godfrey. "Godfrey's Diary, 1862-1873." *The Rhodes Saga*. Transc. Frank Morewood. Self-published, 2006

[2] Glenn Bydwell, from the booklet celebrating 150 years *Tadoussac Protestant Chapel 1866 – 2016* compiled by Susie Bruemmer.

Book of Common Prayer and that was all that was used for the services for several decades. In recent years church liturgies have changed and the increased openness has led to clerical leadership from several different denominations such that we are returning to our original mandate, to be truly non-denominational.

Whoever leads the services, the important tradition that continues is that of the community assembling on Sunday mornings for a summer-length service. It is an opportunity to sit where our ancestors have sat to hear the word of God surrounded by memorials of people from our families. For that reason, it is important for many of our members to have their baptisms, their weddings, and even their memorial services in what has become their ancestral church home.

＆

"They and their children after them shall live there,
And their grandchildren, for all generations."
Ezek. 37:25

MEMORIALS

George Barnston 1800-1883

George Barnston was a hard-working and very intelligent man who worked for the Hudson's Bay Company. It was that work that brought him to Tadoussac late in his career. His strong interest and study in botany and insects were recognized by professionals in those fields.

George Barnston was born in Edinburgh, Scotland, and educated as a surveyor and an army engineer. He joined the North West Company in 1820 (at twenty years old) which united with the Hudson's Bay Company a year later. Barnston started his career as a clerk at York Factory in Manitoba, then transferred to the Columbia District in 1826, where he assisted Amilius Simpson in surveying the Pacific Coast and later helped James McMillan establish Fort Langley (near present-day Langley, B.C.) before serving in two other forts in Washington State.

In 1829 he married Ellen Matthews, a half-native daughter of an American Fur Company employee, and he fathered eleven children. The oldest of these was James who, in 1847, went to Edinburgh for a medical degree.

After a year's furlough in England, Barnston was appointed to Tadoussac in 1844. This was a move that he said made possible "having my children better educated, an object ever near to my heart." It is likely that education took place in Montreal, as Tadoussac would have been a very isolated and undeveloped community at that time. In fact, Barnston described our

George Barnston in Hudson's Bay Coat

beloved village as "an extended, troublesome, and complicated" charge, (as Simpson had warned him it would be); one beset by free traders, smugglers, and encroaching settlement. But it was an opportunity for him to prove his abilities and justify Simpson's confidence in him, and in March 1847 he was promoted to Chief Factor.

He served in Tadoussac for seven years, then later took posts in Manitoba and Ontario before retiring to Montreal in 1863. Retirement freed Barnston to pursue scientific research, primarily in botany and the study of insects - areas in which he had already done a great deal of work in the field and as a writer. Barnston first studied insects at Martin's Falls and kept a journal of the area's temperature, permafrost, flora, and fauna for the Royal Geographical Society of London. He visited several scientific societies on furlough in England in 1843–44. "Finding that I was kindly received at the British Museum," he wrote to George Simpson, "I handed over without reservation all my collection of insects to that institution, at which the gentlemen there expressed high gratification." Over half of his specimens were new to the museum. He later gathered an extensive herbarium at Tadoussac, which he described in his correspondence with Hargrave, and in 1849–50 sent a collection of plants to Scotland. He also supplied specimens to the Smithsonian Institution (Washington, D.C.) and to McGill College.

After 1857 he frequently published articles, mainly in the *Canadian Naturalist and Geologist*. An active member of the Natural History Society of Montreal, he served as its president in 1872–73 and later became a fellow of the Royal Society of Canada in 1882.

It would appear that in his retirement, George Barnston lived in Montreal but spent summers in Tadoussac studying the natural world.

George Barnston died in Montreal in 1883, and the funeral was held at Christ Church Cathedral. The Royal Society of Canada paid tribute to Barnston as both a "diligent naturalist" and "a man of kind and amiable character, loved and respected by all who knew him."

Willis Russell 1814-1887
& Rebecca Page (Sanborn) 1813-1889

Willis Russell came originally from Vermont where he had been associated with his brothers in the paper, pulp, and lumber business. Willis married Rebecca Page (Sanborn) who descended from a long line of early New England colonists. Rebecca's great grandfather, Lieutenant John Sanborn, was born in Norfolk, England in about 1620 and emigrated to the colonies in 1632 with the Rev. Stephen Bachiler party on the ship *William and Frances*, settling in Hampton, New Hampshire, the town having been founded by Rev. Bachiler. Many generations later, Rebecca Page Sanborn was born in 1813 in Sanbornton, NH to John Sanborn and Dorcas Nelson.

Not much is known about Rebecca herself other than she married Willis in Franklin, NH in 1835 and eight years later they relocated to Quebec City where she and Willis lived until 1887 when he died and she died a year later at age seventy-five. An interesting historical note: Rebecca was distantly related to Thomas Nelson Page, the US Ambassador to Italy during the First World War and a direct descendant of the Virginian, Thomas Nelson Jr., a signer of the Declaration of Independence.

Willis and Rebecca had six children: Mary, William, Charles, Ellen, Arthur, and Agnes. Mary and William are the ones whose descendants have continued to come to Tadoussac.

After being sent by his family to Quebec to investigate business opportunities there, Willis remained a resident of Quebec City throughout the rest of his life and found himself in the hotel business, owning the *St. Louis*, the *Albion*, and the *Russell House* (now the *Clarendon*). The missal stand on the chapel altar on which the prayer book rests is made from an oak beam taken from the *St. Louis Hotel* when it was demolished to make room for the *Chateau Frontenac*.

When the doctor recommended sea air for Willis's ailing daughter, his friend Colonel Rhodes of Quebec suggested they try Tadoussac. The two men bought lots beside each other in 1860 so they could continue the friendship of the two families. Rhodes built immediately and

Russell the next year. His order to the builder was "build a house just like William Rhodes's house."

Subsequently, the Ste. Marguerite Salmon Club was founded in 1885 by Willis Russell and Robert Powel of Philadelphia and the three men could adjourn to the Marguerite River for salmon fishing. The Salmon Club leased all the rights on the Marguerite River along which they built six cottages. One of these, known as *Bardsville*, still stands.

A big promoter of Quebec tourism, Willis Russell wrote a book on the history of Quebec which can still be bought on Amazon (*Quebec; as it was and as it is*). Willis Russell was involved with the Tadoussac Hotel and Sea Bathing Company which opened the original hotel in 1864. He lived in Quebec City for forty-five uninterrupted years.

He is buried in Mt. Hermon Cemetery. Susie (Scott) Bruemmer, Willis and Rebecca's great-great-granddaughter, now owns the property known as *Spruce Cliff* near the Tadoussac Tennis Club. The Dewarts, Reilleys, and O'Neills who all spend time in the summer in Tad in their own cottages are also direct descendants of Willis and Rebecca Russell.

Joseph Radford 1815 – 1885
& Isabella (White) 1817-1902

Joseph Radford came to Tadoussac in the 1840s, it is believed from England, and lived in Tadoussac for most of his life with his wife, Isabella White, and his daughter. They are believed to be the only anglophone full-time residents of the town at that time.

Joseph Radford was a prominent citizen in the early days of the town of Tadoussac and had many different jobs. He originally came to work in the Price Sawmill in Anse à l'Eau, but in 1848 William Price closed the mill, and Radford became the manager, in a caretaker role, to occasionally operate the mill when enough wood was harvested. In 1874 the old mill was ceded to the Federal Ministry of Marine Fisheries for $1, and Radford directed the renovation of the old building for its new role, as a fish hatchery, which he managed for the next eleven years.

In 1878, surviving documents show that he was paid $400 for "conducting a fish breeding establishment," and the hatchery raised and released up to a million small salmon a year in the area's rivers.

Mr. Radford was the last Factor of the Hudson's Bay Post, which was located in front of the Hotel Tadoussac until it was demolished in about 1870. He was also listed as Tadoussac's Postmaster, Protection Officer, and Customs Agent, and apparently served as the Swedish and Norwegian Vice-Consul. It is uncertain what that job entailed!

When the group of summer residents, Rhodes, Russell, and Urquhart got together to form a company to build the first *Tadoussac Hotel* in 1864, Joseph Radford was a member of the group. He is also listed as one of the founders of the Tadoussac Protestant Chapel in 1866.

It was in 1863 that he bought the land opposite the *Hotel Georges* from David Price, and demolished the house that was there to build a magnificent white house overlooking the old salmon pool and the cove. Early photos of Anse à l'Eau feature two imposing buildings above the wharf and mill, the *Hotel Georges* (then a residence) and the *Radford House*.

In 1873 there was excitement in Tadoussac. Lord Dufferin was coming to build a house and become a summer resident. Joseph Radford

Radford House at right in Anse a l'Eau

had been a town councillor and by this time was the Mayor of Tadoussac, although the town had not yet been incorporated so he is not listed as the first mayor officially. However, he and the other prominent people in town at the time wrote a flowery letter of welcome, in which they explained that they could not possibly afford to provide a welcoming reception, being such a small community, but "hope that we may have the pleasure during many future seasons of seeing your Excellencies and your amiable family at our beautiful little seaside village."

Joseph Radford died in Tadoussac in 1885 at the age of seventy, and his family continued to live in the house for many years. His unmarried daughter, Belle, inherited the house and lived there until she was too old to manage it, whereupon she sold it to Lady Price in 1918. Belle went to live in Montreal but continued to spend her summers in Tadoussac, staying at the *Hotel Georges* across the street, then known as the *Desmeules Boarding House*. Ainslie Stephen remembered going with her mother, Dorothy Evans, to visit Belle in the years before her death in 1935.

The *Radford House* was used to put up overflow guests from Lady Price's cottage, which was *Fletcher Cottage* by then, and as these guests were mainly relatives and friends of her son, young men home from the First World War, it became known as the "bachelor house". It was destroyed by fire during a strong northwest storm in the winter of 1932.

Alexander Urquhart 1816-1897

Alexander Urquhart was born in Cawdor, Nairnshire, Scotland in 1816. His parents were Mary MacDonald and John Urquhart and he was the eldest in a family of seven children. His two brothers were James Kyle and Charles Calder Mackintosh and his sisters were May, Isabella, Jessie, and Mary.

Alexander came to Canada in June of 1840 and joined the congregation of St. Gabriel Street Presbyterian Church in Montreal, which was then the wealthiest and best-attended church in the city. Shortly after his arrival in Montreal, he went to Quebec City where he lived for four years and was married to Elizabeth Cumming. He returned to Montreal in 1844 and established a business, Alexander Urquhart & Company.

The enterprise started as a wholesale grocery business which grew and diversified over time. The company imported goods from Europe and the Caribbean. Its products were sold in Quebec and Ontario, and in the burgeoning regions of the Canadian northwest – the Red River District and beyond. He was an active member of the congregation of the St. Gabriel Street Church holding the position of treasurer from 1844 to 1846.

Alexander Urquhart

He remained involved in the administration of the church before moving to St. Andrew's Church in 1855. By this time his business had become well-established, and he was a prominent member of the Montreal business community. His Montreal home was on Côte de Neiges just above Sherbrooke Street in the sector known as the Golden Square Mile. His sister May married Alexander Begg, a druggist, of Quebec City and his brother James Kyle came to Canada and was closely associated with Alexander's business interests.

Alexander Urquhart's interest in Tadoussac was most likely kindled through his involvement in the *Tadoussac Hotel and Sea Bathing Company*. The company principals included William Rhodes, Willis Russell, and Joseph Radford. The group built the first *Hotel Tadoussac* which opened its doors in 1864. Urquhart was also one of the founders of the Tadoussac Protestant Chapel which conducted its first protestant services in 1866 on the hotel lawn.

In 1864, Mr. Urquhart purchased the land and buildings above the wharf at Anse à l'Eau from David Price. The land was on the opposite side of the road from a house built in 1863 by his colleague Joseph Radford. Urquhart converted the large square building on the property into a spacious summer home. The redesigned residence included a windowed dome on the roof from which he could keep an eye on the shipping that brought his goods from Montreal to supply the needs of the *Hotel Tadoussac*.

Alexander and Elizabeth Urquhart had three daughters: May, Charlotte, and Mary. The family spent their summers in Tadoussac and the daughters, along with the two sons of Alexander and May Begg, participated in the social functions of the time. Godfrey Rhodes's diary recounts evening dances with the Urquharts at Tadoussac summer residences. The youthful energy levels and late-night antics among the young in Tadoussac have a long history as does the patience of parents and grandparents. Alexander Urquhart continued actively in his business until 1875 when he retired. He died in 1897 in Montreal. The Urquhart family continued to spend their summers in Tadoussac until 1905.

Lieutenant Colonel the Honourable
William Rhodes 1821-1892
& Anne Catherine (Dunn) 1823-1911

William Rhodes was born in 1821, at Bramhope Hall near Leeds, in England. His father, also named William Rhodes, was a wealthy farmer and a soldier who fought for the British in the War of 1812 in Canada. The older William was a Captain in the 19th Lancers, the former 19th Light Dragoons, and married Ann Smith.

Young William was educated in France, and as a second son, he knew that he would not inherit, so his father bought him a commission in the army. He entered the British Army in May 1838 as an ensign in the 68th Foot (Durham Light Infantry).

It was in August of 1841 that twenty-year-old William Rhodes came to Quebec from England as part of a military posting and served in Quebec from October 1842 to May 1844. He fell in love with the land, the river, the people, and eventually with a young lady from Trois Rivieres named Anne Dunn whom he planned to marry.

The older William did not want his son to marry a colonial and pulled strings in the military to have him recalled but William returned and married Anne Dunn in the Anglican Cathedral of the Holy Trinity, Quebec City, in 1847, and left the army with the rank of captain.

Anne Dunn's grandfather, Thomas Dunn had come to Quebec in 1760, a year after General James Wolfe's invasion. He administered Lower Canada from 1805 to 1807, and in 1811. Anne's parents were Robert Dunn, who was an assistant to the Office of Civil Secretary, and Margaret Bell. Her maternal grandfather was Matthew Bell. In 1848, Captain Rhodes and Anne Dunn purchased the estate of *Benmore* on Chemin St. Louis in Sillery, where they settled and engaged in horticulture. The house remained in the Rhodes family for a hundred years and still stands, although today it is part of a condo development. William Rhodes was known for his experimental agriculture, learning what crops and cattle would best tolerate the Quebec environment. During the 1860s he got into business where he associated with Evan John Price and others and engaged with them in mining in the counties

Anne Dunn and Col. William Rhodes finally married!

of Wolfe and Mégantic. He was one of the founders of the Union Bank of Lower Canada and of the Grand Trunk Railway, President of Company Warehouse Quebec and the Quebec Bridge Company which eventually built the first Quebec Bridge. He led a delegation on April 12, 1888, to meet Sir John A. Macdonald and Sir Charles Tupper to lobby for funds to build the bridge. He helped to establish the Quebec and Richmond Railway and the North Shore Line, which later merged with the CPR.

In politics, Rhodes was the MP for Megantic from 1854 to 1857. Later, he joined the Mercier cabinet as Minister of Agriculture and Colonization and was elected Liberal MP for Mégantic in the Legislative Assembly in a by-election in 1888.

During this time, William and Anne produced five sons and four daughters over a twenty-year period and they were very eager that all of their children be educated and guided into a successful future. Rhodes was an avid hunter and outdoorsman, and the boys were taken on lengthy camping trips in the winter with friends, often returning to Quebec City with sleds loaded with enough game to provision the household for two months.

The daughters in the family were not neglected in their education. In one of his many letters to the family in England, he wrote: "… the little girls have now music, dancing, and French masters, to say nothing of sewing machines, pudding making, and English writing. In fact, tuition and all its branches are the order of the day."

It was through his friendship with the lumber merchant Price family that William Rhodes first discovered Tadoussac. A businessman and politician at heart, it wasn't long before he was taking leadership here too. He built the anglophone community's first summer cottage in 1860, and his friends in the Russell family, also of Quebec City, built an exact copy right next door which is still in the Russell family—*Spruce Cliff* owned by Susie (Scott) Bruemmer. William Rhodes's cottage would have looked exactly like that at first, but then he extended it to accommodate his growing family and it burned down in 1932. *Brynhyfryd* is the second cottage, built in the same location.

Robert Hale Powel was another friend who decided to build a summer cottage in Tadoussac. He bought the next lot, currently the Baileys. It is said the three friends, Rhodes, Russell, and Powel often played whist together. Perhaps it was during such a game that the opportunity was either offered or asked for that William's sons, Armitage and Godfrey, move to Philadelphia to work in one of Powel's rolling mills. The boys got experience like any other worker on the machine shop floors where the manual labour was hot and hard. They gradually moved up the ranks learning every aspect of the trade until they became executives in their own right, as leaders in the rail business.

William Rhodes and Mr. Russell were part of a group that built the original *Hotel Tadoussac* in 1864, and it was in a meeting in that new hotel that they committed themselves to building the Protestant Chapel in 1866. His son Godfrey kept a diary that records camping trips when they would row locally built nor'shore canoes up to Baie St. Etienne to camp and fish. But for all the forays out into the wilds, William remained devoted to his first and only love. He wrote of Anne: "… I find her a valuable assistant, in interpreting to me the characters of the young men I have to deal with. (…) Few women have performed all their duties to their children so well and so unceasingly as my wife".

For all his work in business and politics, William Rhodes was a devoted father and, judging by photographs that have survived, he and Anne were lovers of their time with family in Tadoussac. One summer he wrote to a family member: "My family is all down at the seaside at Tadoussac. We are all together which is a great comfort, far preferable to having sons away in India or floating about the ocean on His Majesty's ships."

Lt Colonel William Rhodes died at Benmore on February 17th, 1892, at the age of seventy. His death was quite unexpected. He had been well but took sick with La Grippe. After the funeral, celebrated in the Anglican Church of St. Michael, he was buried in Mount Hermon Cemetery.

The Rhodeses had nine children and twenty grandchildren, all of whom spent significant time in Tadoussac, so it is worthwhile recording some of the descendants here.

William's wife Anne (Dunn) Rhodes outlived the Colonel by twenty years, and it is said that she was a sweet lady; however, with so many grandchildren she became a bit vague as to which child was which. Just imagine the struggle she would have in keeping her descendants straight today!

The oldest son was Armitage, and his daughter Dorothy (Dorsh) married Trevor Evans. Their children are Phoebe, Ainslie, Trevor, and Tim, producing nine more Evans, Skutezkys, and Stevens.

Next was Godfrey, who bought the estate *Cataraqui* in Quebec. He had two daughters: Gertrude who died in infancy; and Catherine, who married Percival Tudor-Hart and lived at the estate until her death in 1972. Godfrey built the *Tudor-Hart Cottage* in Languedoc Park here in Tadoussac. There are no descendants.

The third son was William. His daughter Carrie would marry her first cousin, Frank. William and Godfrey had been sent to the United States to work in the railway business, so they lived in the US and William travelled around the world building railways.

The fourth son, Francis, married a Quebec girl, Totie Le Moine, from *Spencer Grange*, another old house that's still standing in Quebec – currently the official residence of the Lieutenant-Governor. Their two surviving daughters (of four) were Lily Bell and Frances, whom many of us remember fondly. Neither married nor had children.

The fifth son was Robert Dunn Rhodes who settled in the United States and had eight children who led to Rhodes, Johnson, and Robes descendants who settled in the Boston area.

The sixth child, and first girl, was Minnie Rhodes. She married Harry Morewood, an American, and they had five children including Frank Morewood who married his first cousin, William's daughter, Carrie. It was Frank and Carrie who built *Windward Cottage* in 1936 and the Evans and Belton families are descendants. William's other children were Isobel, known as Billy, John, and Nancy as well as Bobby who had two sons, Frank and Harry Morewood.

Seventh, there was Nan who married Lennox Williams. Their children were: James, who was killed in World War I; Mary, the matriarch of the Wallace and Leggat families; Gertrude, who led to the Alexander and Aylan-Parker families; and Sydney, whose descendants include the Williams, Ballantynes, Websters, and Campbells.

The eighth and ninth children were Fanny who died in infancy and Gertrude, who married, but died childless at twenty-six years old.

Robert Hare Powel 1825-1883
& Amy Smedley (Bradley) 1825-1908

The Powel family came from Pennsylvania. Robert's father - John Powel Hare (1786-1856) was an American agriculturist, politician, art collector, and philanthropist. He was born John Powel Hare and was adopted by his mother's widowed and childless sister, Elizabeth Willing Powel. He legally changed his name to John Hare Powel when he attained his majority and inherited the immense fortune of his late uncle, Samuel Powel. He was educated at The Academy and College of Philadelphia and after college joined a counting house. As part of his job in mercantile affairs, he travelled to Calcutta and returned at age twenty-two with $22,000 as his share of the profit.

Robert's mother, Julia (De Veaux), was the daughter of Colonel Andrew De Veaux. She and John married in 1817. They had seven children: Samuel, De Veaux, Henry Baring, Robert Hare, Julia, John Hare Jr., and Ida. The couple and their young family lived on the Powel family farmland known as *Powelton*, in west Philadelphia, where John began efforts to improve American agriculture.

Robert Hare Powel married Amy Smedley (Bradley) who had been born in 1825, in Chester, Pennsylvania. Together they had six children: Julia De Veaux (1851), William Platt (1853 who only lived one year) Robert Hare jr. (1857), Amy Ida (1858), De Veaux (1861) and Henry Baring (1864).

Robert and Amy purchased land in Tadoussac in 1865 from Willis Russell and built a house next door to him (The Bailey house). The adjoining lots were connected by a gate and Mrs. Powel visited Mrs. Russell nearly every afternoon. These Rhodes, Russell, and Powel properties were referred to as "our three cottages" by the men and the three of them often played whist together in the evening. Mr. Powel was said to be "the life of every party" and they were very generous and hospitable to young people from Tadoussac who visited them in Philadelphia, not least some of Col. Rhodes's sons who worked in Mr. Powel's rail yards.

Both Robert Powel and Willis Russell were charter members of

The Powel's Hillcrest

the Marguerite Salmon Club. There were a number of other charter members, all American, Willis Russell being the only Canadian.

Robert died in 1883. His obituary, taken from The Daily News of Huntingdon, Pennsylvania, describes his activities during his career.

> *"Robert Hare Powel, the great coal operator, died suddenly at Saxton, Bedford County, on Monday evening last. His death was caused by indigestion ... On Monday morning he was unable to get up and continued to grow worse until about 7 o'clock in the evening when he expired. Dr. Brumbaugh, of this place, had been summoned, but the train did not arrive at Saxton until five minutes after Mr. Powel died... The intelligence of his sudden death was received here the same evening, and could scarcely be believed, as he had been well on Saturday and was in the best of health.*
>
> *Mr. Powel's loss will be greatly felt in this section. He was the first to penetrate the semi-bituminous coal region in this county and the first to ship the coal to the east. He continued to develop not only the vast deposits of coal but of iron and while wealth accumulated as the result of his foresight and sagacity, he sought other channels for investing his means, thereby giving employment to thousands of workmen.*
>
> *He was honest and honourable in business transactions, plain and unassuming in manner, a self-made man."*

His widow and family continued to come to Tadoussac in the summers and it wasn't until 1906, a year before Amy's death, that the house was sold to Sam and Alfred Piddington.

Amelia Jane (LeMesurier) Smith 1832-1917

Amelia Jane LeMesurier was born in Quebec City in 1832. She was the fourth daughter and one of twelve children of Henry LeMesurier and his wife Julie Guerout. In 1857 she married Robert Herbert Smith (1825-1898) also of Quebec City. He was involved in the Timber and Shipping business, and it is this business that may have brought the family to Tadoussac.

They had eight children, Robert Harcourt (1858), Edith (1862, who married Henry Baring Powel), Amelia Blanche (1863, who married Sir William Price), Herbert (1866), Charles (1867), George (1870), Edmund (1874), and Arthur (1875). There are memorial plaques for all these children except Edith.

Amelia's oldest son, Harcourt, was also in the lumber business and he bought *Dufferin House* from the Dale family. It may have been he who brought the Smith family to Tadoussac, currently in its sixth generation.

Amelia Jane died in Quebec City in 1917 having been predeceased by her sons Robert Harcourt in 1913 and Herbert in 1915. She is buried with her husband in Mount Hermon Cemetery, in Quebec City.

Because these are the first Smiths to come to Tadoussac it is worth noting here that first, it is unknown whether Amelia's husband Robert ever holidayed here. It may be that Amelia and her other children only came after her son Harcourt bought *Dufferin House* in 1911. Also, because Amelia Blanche married Sir William Price, and Edith married Henry Baring Powel, the Smith, Price and Powel families became connected. Coosie Price, Harky Powel and brothers Lex, Gordon and Guy Smith were all first cousins. It should be noted that the name Carington is not part of the Smith surname, but a frequently used middle name.

Amelia Smith with son Harcourt and grandson Gordon

Henry Ferrier Price 1833-1898

Henry Price was born at Wolfesfield in Sillery, Quebec, the Price family estate acquired by his father, William Price, who had arrived from Wales in 1810. William had begun wood-cutting operations on the Saguenay River that would later become Price Brothers. Henry was the fourth son of William and Jane Stewart, who was descended from Scottish supporters of Bonnie Prince Charlie. They had fourteen children. Henry's brothers David Edward, Evan John and William Evan took over the company from their father, but Henry had other plans.

Henry decided to travel to California to join the Gold Rush. He boarded a ship and sailed south around Cape Horn. Upon reaching Chile in 1850 on the voyage north he visited with his Uncle Richard who had settled there. His uncle persuaded him to abandon his plans and he stayed in Chile where he worked in his uncle's business of cattle and horses.

In 1866 Henry married Florence Stoker Rogerson who was born in Ireland in 1841. They settled on their *"Estancia"* in Talcahuano, Chile where all seven of their children were born: William, Henry Edward, Teresa Jane (Aunt Terry), Arthur John, Florence Mary (Aunt Flo Bradshaw), Frederick Courtnay, and Lewellyn.

Henry's brothers back home in Canada had remained bachelors and urged him to come home so that they could keep the lumber business in the family. He sent his oldest sons, William and Henry Edward, north in 1879 to finish their high school education and apprentice in the business. In 1884 Henry Ferrier and the rest of his family moved to Canada and settled in Toronto. The children were sent to different schools as they matured. Henry Edward went to Trinity College in Port Hope as did Arthur. Fred and Lewellyn were sent to Ridley College in St Catherine's.

William, the eldest, was sent to BCS in Lennoxville, Quebec for a year before going to school in England. He would later take over building Price Brothers and was knighted (Sir William) for his work with the Canadian Army during World War I.

In Tadoussac, William rebuilt *Fletcher Cottage* for his family and a house nearby called *Casa Nueva* which later became the *Harry Price House*. Henry Ferrier died in Toronto in 1898 and is buried in Mt. Pleasant Cemetery. His wife, Florence, died in 1921 and is buried beside him.

Frances (MacIntosh) Watt d. 1876 & David A. Watt d. 1918

There is a window at the back of the church dedicated to the memory of Frances MacIntosh Watt but there is little known about her. We know she died on July 1, 1876, and that she was buried in Outremont, Montreal, Quebec at the Mont-Royal Cemetery.

The tombstone is inscribed:
FRS. MACINTOSH wife of DAVID A. WATT
DIED 1ST JULY 1876
NEIL MACINTOSH, BROTHER
ISABELLA McLEAN, cousin

Her husband was originally named David Allan Poe and apparently changed his name to Watt. He went by Poe in the 1861 census and when he was married to Frances in 1857. However, he signed as D. A. P. Watt on the original chapel subscriber's list of 1866. David and Frances had four children, three girls, and a boy, but even in David's obituary below the girls are not identified by name. He seems to have died in 1918, suggesting that Frances was much younger when she died over forty years before, but her date of birth is unknown.

Mr. David Allan Watt Passed Away in his 88th Year
The death of Mr. David Allan Watt took place last Thursday at his residence, 285 Stanley Street. He was born in Ayrshire, Scotland, in 1830, and was thus eighty-eight years of age. He was educated at the Grammar School, Greenock, came to Canada in 1846, and was one of the organizers of the Corn Exchange, the Citizen's League, and the Montreal Art Association. He was the editor of the Canadian Naturalist. In 1857 he married Miss Frances Macintosh, his wife predeceasing him in 1876. He is survived by his four children, Mrs. F. H. Whitmore and the Misses Watt, of Montreal, and Mr. Allan Watt, of Rocky Mount, N. C.

The Very Reverend Thomas Frye Lewis Evans 1846-1919
Marie Stewart (Bethune) 1850-1903
Emily Elizabeth (Bethune) 1866-1947
Cyril Lewis Evans 1882-1887

The Very Reverend Thomas Frye Lewis Evans served as a summer minister in Tadoussac for thirty-five years back between about 1884 and his death in 1919. He married Marie Stewart Bethune and with her had five children, Basil (1873), Muriel (1877) Trevor (1879), Cyril (1882), and Ruby (1885).

Little is known about Marie except that she was said to have been a lively and engaging woman and usually called May. She married Lewis Evans in 1873 at the age of twenty-three. She is named Maria in her birth record, and Marie in the marriage index, (and Marie on her plaque). Her full name was Maria Stewart Bethune, born in 1850, the second of four children (all girls) of Strachan Bethune (1821-1910) and Maria MacLean Phillips (1826-1901). She died in 1903 and is buried in Mount Royal Cemetery.

Included in that list of Marie's children is Cyril who died at five years old. There is a small window in the back wall of the chapel that is dedicated to the memory of Cyril Lewis Evans. He died of hydrocephalus at the age of five. It is hard to imagine now how that tragedy played out, the little boy dying in 1887.

Hydrocephalus (sometimes called water on the brain) can cause brain damage as a result of fluid buildup. This can lead to developmental, physical, and intellectual impairments caused by Cerebrospinal fluid (CSF) which flows through the brain and spinal cord under normal conditions. Under certain conditions, the amount of this fluid in the brain increases if there is a blockage that prevents it from flowing normally, or if the brain produces an excess amount of it.

In the 1880s treatment for this condition was in its infancy, so it must have been a very difficult time for Cyril and his family.

After Marie's death, the Dean married her cousin, Emily Elizabeth

Back Row: Basil, Dean Evans, Trevor, R. Lewis (aged 7)
Front Row: Emily, Kay, Miles Hudspeth, Muriel

Bethune (1866-1947), and had one more child, Robert Lewis Evans (1911) when he was about sixty-five years old, and Emily was forty-five.

This family was not connected to any of the other summer cottage families until son Trevor, and later son Lewis married into the Rhodes family, and both had cottages in Tadoussac.

Dean Evans was the rector of St. Stephen's Church in Montreal, a church on Atwater Street, and stayed there for forty-six years. While there, he served as an Honourary Canon, Archdeacon, and then was named the fifth Dean of Montreal Diocese but would only accept the position if he could stay at St. Stephen's and not move over to the Cathedral. In 1908 he was within a whisker of being elected Bishop. It was an actual split vote and they had to adjourn for three weeks to sort it out in typical Anglican political manoeuvring. They picked the other guy, John Craig Farthing. The Dean died in 1919. It is said that he had pneumonia, collapsed in the pulpit on a Sunday morning while delivering his sermon, and died a few days later.

Very few of Dean Lewis Evans's writings remain but it is clear from them that he was a devoted churchman and that he had worked hard to help in the development of the Anglican Diocese of Montreal. A school in the St. Henri district was named after him, and he was very insistent that all of the Anglican clergy should be able to speak French. In Tadoussac, he lived in what was then the furthest east Price house, the Beattie/Price house. It was built along with the other Price houses for the administrators of Price Brothers Lumber, but this one was lent to Dean Evans and he eventually acquired it by squatter's rights. From him, it passed to his wife, Emily Elizabeth (Bethune) Evans, and then to their son, Lewis Evans, who sold it to James and Anne Beattie. The Dean had also owned a part of the tennis club property which he bought from the Price family, but he sold his portion to Jonathan Dwight and Mr. Dwight sold it to the tennis club.

Dean Evans was an avid fisherman and had built for himself a small log cabin about nine miles up the Saguenay on the west side of the river at a place called Cap à Jack. It seemed he needed a cottage to get away from his cottage! He had a little powerboat called *Minota* which he would take up there towing a couple of nor'shore canoes to fish out of. One of the local men, André Nicolas, in speaking about the Dean, said he had seen photos of the fishing camp on the website, tidesoftadoussac. com, that grandson Tom Evans set up. He said that where Lewis Evans had his camp was, and still is, the best place on the river to catch sea trout. It is interesting, a hundred years later, to hear a local fisherman say that the Dean got it right!

Frank & John Morewood, Lily Bell & Frances Rhodes with their father Francis,
Dorothy Rhodes & her father Armitage, with Nancy Morewood & Catherine
& Charile Rhodes in front, picnicking at the sand dunes

Armitage Rhodes 1848-1909
& Phoebe Ida (Alleman) 1854-1893

Armitage Rhodes was born in 1848 at *Benmore* (Sillery) Quebec, the eldest son of Col. William Rhodes and Anne Catherine Dunn. A Civil Engineer, (and founding member of the Society of Engineers of Quebec), he was educated at Bishop's College School and in Philadelphia, U.S.A. He enjoyed camping, hunting, boating, and fishing. As a young man, he sang in the choir of the Tadoussac chapel.

His first wife was Phoebe Ida Alleman who was born in Pennsylvania in 1854, the daughter of Frederick O. Alleman and Mary B. Alleman (born Oglesby). Their children were Mathew Charles Kingsley Rhodes (adopted) and his daughter Dorothy Gwendolyn Esther Rhodes who was born in 1892. Ida was a prolific amateur painter. Several of her oil portraits, sea, and landscapes survive to this day in family hands. She died in 1893, in Sillery, Quebec at age thirty-nine.

Armitage subsequently married Catherine von Iffland and their two daughters were Monica Rhodes and Armitage (Peter) Rhodes. Monica never married, and Armitage (who was given male-sounding names because her father had wanted a boy!) was the mother of Ann Hargreaves (Cumyn).

Like his father William, Armitage senior was a prominent Quebec City businessman and served as President and Chairman of several companies including Quebec Warehousing Corporation, the Quebec Bridge Corporation, a director of the Union Bank, and the Grand Trunk Railway. He served as president of the Royal Literary and Historical Society.

Armitage brought his family to the Rhodes family cottage in Tadoussac for many summers that they spent with the rest of the Rhodes family.

The memorial plaque in the chapel lists the names and dates of Armitage and his first wife, as well as his daughter, Dorothy, and her husband, Trevor Evans.

Henry Dale 1849-1910
& Katrine Dale d. 1905

Henry Dale was an American, born in Philadelphia, the son of Gerald Fitzgerald Dale (1816-1886) and a direct descendant of Governor Dale of Delaware. His mother was Elizabeth (Sparhawk) Dale (1820-1907).

Henry married Elizabeth Ramsen Keroy and became the third owner of *Dufferin House* which he referred to as *The Cottage*. His gardens were above the house where the school now stands, and probably the stables were there also.

He also owned land extending from the eastern boundary of Dwight Park out to Pointe Rouge, much of which is now known as Languedoc Park. (The stone gate in front of the Evans' *Windward Cottage* was the original entrance to Dwight Park which extended up the hill to Languedoc Park.) The road into the park opposite the farm was known as Dale Road.

Henry Dale had a carriage road going down to Pointe Rouge where, with horse and carriage, he is said to have circled the "fairy circle" each morning and returned home for breakfast. While Henry owned the park, he planted alder bushes to prevent erosion and to provide shelter for other seedlings.

After the tragic death of their daughter, Katrine, at age seventeen in 1905, the Dales stopped coming to Tadoussac and in 1911, a year after Henry's death, his estate sold *Dufferin House* to Robert Harcourt Carington Smith. In 1920 Mrs. Dale sold the land above Pointe Rouge for $1,400 to Erie Russell Janes (wife of George de Guerry Languedoc) who designed and built *Amberley*, the cottage later purchased by Adelaide Gomer of Ithaca, New York.

Henry Dale died in Poughkeepsie, N.Y. in 1910. He was described in his obituary as a Philadelphia and New York businessman. He belonged to the Aldine and Lawyers' Club of New York and the Union League Club of Philadelphia. He died at his home which was called *The Hemlocks*.

William Edward Russell 1849-1893
& Fanny Eliza (Pope) 1856-1936

William Edward Russell, son of Willis Russell and Rebecca Page Sanborn, was born in Quebec in 1849. As a child in Tad in his mid-teens, William (Willy) was a playmate of his neighbour, Godfrey Rhodes, Colonel Rhodes's son, and many of their teenage exploits are detailed in Godfrey's diary.

Fanny Eliza Pope, the wife of William Edward Russell, was born in Chatham, England, in 1856. Her father, Lieutenant Colonel James Pope, later became the commander of the English army stationed in Quebec and at some point, her paths crossed with William's, and they married at Trinity Cathedral in Quebec in 1874 - Fanny being then the tender age of eighteen. William Edward inherited the hotel business from his father, Willis, but unfortunately, William was not much of a businessman and died practically insolvent six years after his father's death – a death that left Fanny Eliza as a young widow of thirty-seven with five children - at least three of whom (Florence Louisa "Nonie" Russell, Willis Robert Russell, and Mabel Emily Russell) continued summering at Tad. It was Fanny Eliza Pope's sister, Louisa Floriana Pope, that later had a profound effect on her goddaughter and grandniece, Ann Stevenson, future wife of the Rev. Russell Dewart.

As Ann Stevenson relates in her book, *Nose to the Window*, Louisa, or "Auntie Totie" as she was called, was born in Malta in about 1852, where her father, Colonel James Pope, was stationed with the British Army.

"As the sole surviving member of the older generation, Auntie Totie was the arbiter of speech and manners. When the Dionne Quints were born and no one knew how to pronounce this strange new word, 'Quintuplets,' she announced that the accent should be on the first syllable. Like most Victorians, she idolized the Royal Family, and it was she who always proposed the toast to the King at Christmas dinner. After she had said grace, we would all stand with her and say "The King! God Bless Him!" and drink to his health. However, because Auntie Totie's name was Pope, and because Mum was particularly fond of the tail of the turkey, known derisively in Protestant England as the Pope's nose, when Dad carved the turkey, he would turn to Mum and say, "Nonie, do you want the Pope's nose?" We would have to stifle our giggles with our napkins and try not to look at Auntie Totie."

Louisa died in Quebec in 1934 and her sister, Fanny Eliza, died two years later in Toronto.

Julia De Veaux (Powel) Peters 1851-1904

Julia was born in 1851, in Pennsylvania, to Robert Hare Powel and Amy Smedley Powel. She was the oldest of six children. Her family lived in Philadelphia and spent time in Quebec City and during the summer, in Tadoussac. Julia's father was a good friend of William Rhodes and Willis Russell, and he built the house that later became the Bailey's.

Julia was the same age as Godfrey and William Rhodes and William Russell, and they spent some happy years growing up together. Their family houses in Tadoussac were in a row next to each other. Julia was very popular and outgoing. The boys led an active outdoor life, boating, and fishing, and she would join them, rowing up the Saguenay and sometimes camping overnight at St Etienne. (The girls had their own tent!)

In the evenings when the young gathered at the Powel's or Russell's houses for dancing and singing, Julia was featured doing waltzes, gallops, and the "jig" with the group. At a Grand Concert and Charade held at the Tadoussac Hotel on July 22, 1870, Julia was one of the performers along with Godfrey Rhodes, Jim Gordon, and Pete Meredith.

Julia was actively involved with the Tadoussac Chapel and sang in the choir on Sundays with Godfrey and Willie. When her family was in Quebec City she joined in the social life of parties and teas, came for dinner at *Cataraqui*, and played cards in the evenings with the Rhodes, and Russells. One day, according to Godfrey, "she drove the cart like a bird and broke a shaft, jamming it at St. John's Gate".

Julia married Samuel Winslow Miller Peters from Virginia in 1874 at age twenty-two, in Pennsylvania. Samuel was born in July 1847, in Virginia, United States. They had two daughters: Mary Louisa Miller Peters (1876), and Amy Powel Peters (1882).

Robert Peel William Campbell 1853-1929

Robert Peel William Campbell was born in St. Hilaire Québec in 1853. He was the second son of Major Thomas Edmund Campbell, seigneur of Rouville, and his wife Henriette-Julie Juchereau Duchesnay. Thomas Campbell became seigneur upon his wife's inheritance of the seigneury from her father, Ignace-Michel-Louis-Antoine d'Irumberry de Salaberry. Robert's great uncle was Charles de Salaberry, CB, who led the Canadian troops at the Battle of Chateauguay in their defeat of a numerically superior American army advancing on Montreal during the War of 1812.

Robert grew up in the *Manoir Rouville*, a Tudor-style mansion located on the south bank of the Richelieu River, in the shadow of majestic Mount St. Hilaire. His youth would have been spent exploring the countryside of St. Hilaire and helping his father with the development of his 150-acre model farm, a large portion of which was devoted to the nurturing of trees. Owing to his mother's French-Canadian roots and his father's British heritage, he was completely fluent in both English and French. This ability would serve him well later in his life.

He attended Bishop's College School in Lennoxville. He continued his studies at the University of Bishop's College completing a Bachelor of Arts degree in June of 1873 and a Masters of Arts degree in June of 1876. At the age of twenty-two, this was quite an accomplishment for the day. He went on to study law at Laval University and with the completion of his L.L.B. was awarded the Dufferin Gold Medal. The medal was an official British commendation awarded by the then Governor-General, Lord Dufferin, to Canadian students who had achieved high excellence in academics and athletics.

While at BCS he would have met boys with ties to Tadoussac. Colonel Rhodes's boys were all around his age and because Robert's father, Thomas, and William Rhodes were both officers in the British Army in Canada at one time in their lives, it is entirely possible that there were family ties before the BCS days. Robert became a great friend of the Rhodes and Williams families and spent many summers visiting their summer home on the banks of Tadoussac Bay. One can imagine these young men leaving Québec on a steamer bound for Tadoussac with the entire summer ahead filled with outdoor adventure on the Saguenay River. Robert was called to the Québec Bar in 1877 and practised law in Québec City. He was appointed Assistant Clerk of the Legislative Council of the Province of Québec in 1883. The Legislative Council was the unelected upper house of the legislature in the province from 1867 to its disbandment in 1968. Concurrently, he was appointed English Journal and English Translator for the Council, no doubt because of his proficiency in both languages. In 1893, he was appointed Clerk of Private Bills and Railways for the Province. He became Clerk of the Legislative Council in 1909. The title of King's Counsel was conferred upon him in 1903.

At some time between 1882 and 1885, Robert purchased the property known as *Kirk Ella* from John Burstall. The eighty-three-acre property was located on the opposite side of Rue St. Louis from Godfrey Rhodes' residence *Cataraqui*. The house on the property was destroyed by fire in 1879 after Burstall had done extensive renovations. A new residence would have been built by Robert Campbell. He lived at *Kirk Ella* until his death.

Robert Campbell never married. Throughout his life, he was devoted to the institutions which were responsible for his education and to the church. For many years he was a member of the Board of Directors of the University of Bishop's College. He took a leading role in the administration of the affairs of the University. In 1907 and in recognition of his many years of service he was awarded the degree of Honorary Doctorate of Laws by the University. He was also Chairman of the Board of Directors of BCS from 1908 to 1912 and a Trustee of King's Hall Compton.

It was probably through his association with the Anglican Church in Québec that he came to be such good friends with Lennox Williams and his wife Nan. Robert became Chancellor and secretary of the Diocese of Québec in 1905 and had been associated with the church in Québec for many years. While six years older than Lennox Williams, Robert would have known him and his father James at BCS, and certainly would have developed a close bond while Lennox was the minister at St. Matthew's Anglican Church in Québec City.

Robert died at *Kirk Ella* in Québec City in 1929. The stories of his time in Tadoussac are lost to the passage of time. The plaque placed in his memory in the Chapel recognizes his long and dedicated service to the Province of Québec, his university, his church, and the great esteem with which he was held by the summer residents of Tadoussac of that generation.

Lieutenant-Colonel Frederick Whitley d. 1914 & Jessie (Chouler) d. 1940 & daughter Jessie Margaret Whitley d. 1882

Most of us who attend services at the chapel have probably read the inscription beneath the front windows hundreds of times. It is both sad and funny. Read by itself, the left-hand window reads "To the Glory of God ... died at Tadoussac, August" which may draw a smile to the faces of the faithful who never subscribed to the "God is Dead" movement of the 1960s. But to read across the three windows as we are expected to do, we learn of a baby who died in 1882 at the age of five months. There is sadness, and we can only wonder, well over a century later, about the reason for the child's death and the sorrow it must have inflicted on the family and friends, particularly on her parents.

Jessie Margaret was born on February 27th and baptized on April 7th of the same year in which she died. She was named after her mother and maternal grandmother, though the family called her Daisy. She died on August 3rd in Tadoussac and was buried on August 5th in Montreal.

Her father was Frederick Whitley who was the son of John Whitley and Sophie Hardy of La Solitude, St. Martin's Parish, Jersey, Channel Islands. It is not known what year he was born, but he was educated at Victoria College, St. Helier's, Jersey, and in Dijon, France, and came to Montreal around 1873. Frederick was first employed in the firm of Thomas Samuel and Company, then established his own firm: Fred'k, Whitley, and Co. Leather Importers, importing high-quality leather mostly from England.

He served as an officer in the Montreal Garrison Artillery and was later transferred to the Montreal Squadron of Cavalry (about 1896), which became the Duke of York's Royal Canadian Hussars. He was also very interested in the work of the Church of England, was a Lay Reader in the Diocese of Montreal, and was Superintendent of St. Martin's and St. James the Apostle Sunday schools.

Frederick returned to England in 1877 to marry Jessie Chouler and brought her back to Canada with him. She was the daughter of Christopher Chouler and Margaret Wilson of London, England.

Her father, Christopher Chouler, was a member of the firm Howell's, Drapers, St. Paul's Churchyard, London. He was the son of Christopher and Mary Chouler, Falcon Lodge, Althorp Park, Northampton. (That Christopher, Jessie's grandfather, was the Estate Manager of Althorp, Princess Diana Spencer's family estate.)

Together, Frederick and Jessie had five children: Frederick, Henry, Ernest, Elsie and Jessie.

Frederick Whitley became an Anglican priest, married, and had one daughter, Ruth, who never married. It was in about 1941 that he gave the brass candlesticks on the altar to the chapel in memory of his parents. Frederick died in 1914, just before World War I and his wife Jessie died in 1940.

Ernest joined his father in business. He married Gertrude McGill and had one daughter, Barbara Jane Whitley, who was never married. She was well-known at the Montreal General Hospital where she volunteered for sixty years. She also started the Whithearn Foundation, a family foundation that was set up to fund research on diseases and disorders of the eye. Barbara passed away at the age of one hundred in 2018 but remembered Tadoussac very well and provided this family information just before she died.

Henry also worked with his father. He and his wife had one daughter Phyllis Rosamond, who married Ralph Collyer and had three children – John, Peter, and Jane (Wandell). Phyllis passed away in 2002, in her ninety-first year at St. Lambert, Quebec. Her daughter, Jane Wandell, is currently a director of the above-mentioned Whithearn Foundation which her aunt, Barbara Whitley, founded.

Elsie married C.S. Bann and had one child, Joan, who married Gordon Rutherford and had one child - Hugh.

The youngest child was Jessie, usually called Daisy, whom we remember in the chapel's front windows.

Harcourt Smith with sons Gordon and Guy

Robert Harcourt Carington Smith 1858-1913 & Mary Valliere (Gunn) 1865-1931

Harky, as he was known, was born in Quebec City in 1858, and was the eldest son of Robert Herbert Smith and Amelia Jane LeMesurier.

He was educated at Bishop College School, in Lennoxville. He was a keen sportsman his whole life, winning many events in local sports and participating in the Thistle Lacrosse League, Quebec Snowshoe Club, and the Quebec Golf Club. In business, he was a partner in the square timber and lumber firm of J. and W. Sharples and Co. and was recognized as one of the ablest and most reliable lumber merchants in Canada.

According to his obituary, "He was a man of unusual business acumen and was devoted to his firm's interest as well as his family." In 1894 he married Mary Valliere Gunn of Kingston, Ontario. They had four sons (Eric who died in infancy), Alexander (Lex) born in 1895, Gordon, born in 1906, and Guy, born in 1908.

In 1911 he purchased *Dufferin House* from the Dale family, and thus began the long history of the Smith family in Tadoussac. Harky died in 1913 of pneumonia at the age of fifty-four. He is buried in Mount Hermon Cemetery in Quebec City.

Alfred Piddington 1859-1922

Alfred Piddington was born in 1859. He came to Tadoussac originally because his sister, Eliza Ernestine Piddington, and her husband, Dr G. G. Gale of Quebec City, had been coming here since the 1880s, renting the old Ferguson house. It is believed that Alfred, and his brother Sam, both bachelors, came to Tadoussac to visit their sister, and fell in love with the area.

The Piddington family originally came from the Isle of Jersey on the English Channel. They immigrated to Quebec in the 19th century and invested in companies like the Quebec-Lake St John Railroad, the Canadian Rubber Company, Sun Life Insurance, the Royal Electric Company, and the Quebec Steamship Company.

In 1906, Sam and Alfred bought a house they called *Hillcrest* following the death of the owner Robert Powel's widow in 1905. This house had originally been called Ivanhoe, and at this writing is known as the Bailey's house. The Powels, from Philadelphia, had built the house in 1865 having obtained the land from Willis Russell of Quebec, both of whom were charter members of the St Marguerite Salmon Club. The Salmon Club, *Hillcrest*, and the Protestant Chapel were built in the Gothic Revival architecture style, which was popular during the 1860s in Canada.

Sam and Alfred were avid sportsmen, enjoying fishing, and hunting in particular. They made changes in the house that reflected these interests. For example, a wall was removed to create a large central room that would become a billiard room, and in that room, they mounted the spoils of their hunting trips, including a stuffed wooden duck, a brace of grouse, and a moose head. Other additions included a player piano and gothic-style chairs.

Sometime between 1906 and 1914, Alfred went on to live in what is now the Stephen-Skutezky house. After his death in 1922, it was bought by Trevor Evans and is maintained by his descendants. Alfred called this house *Ivanhoe*, the original name for *Hillcrest*. It's interesting that many items in both houses are similar including furniture, a piano, a brace of grouse, and even a moose head on the wall.

Many old family photographs show that the Piddingtons and the Gales enjoyed sailing on the yacht *Pirate* and picnicking in various places up the Saguenay. Many pictures show them enjoying recreational activities on the *Hillcrest* lawn, which then extended to the *Dufferin House* property, where the school is today. They enjoyed lawn bowling, lawn tennis, cricket, croquet, and horseback riding. He even made a miniature golf course. The family still has a picture of Alfred Piddington playing golf in the early days of the Tadoussac Golf Club. In addition, their original guestbook records the names of many summer residents who attended elaborate tea parties at *Hillcrest*.

Alfred's brother, Sam Piddington, died in 1925 and left *Hillcrest* to his beloved niece, Ernestine Valiant Gale Bailey and it has been in the Bailey family ever since.

Besides the memorial plaque in the Chapel, large cottonwood trees, nearly one hundred years old and unusual for this region, were planted in memory of Sam, Alfred, and Eliza Piddington, in front of *Hillcrest*, facing the bay.

Erie Russell (Janes) 1863-1941
& George de Guerry Languedoc 1860-1924

Erie Russell Janes (b. 1863 in Montreal) was the daughter of Mary Frances (Russell) and her husband, William D. B. Janes. Soon after her sister's birth in 1864, Erie's mother died and she went to Quebec to live with her grandparents, Willis Russell, and his wife, Rebecca Page Sanborn. Willis Russell, her grandfather, was one of the first Quebec residents to build a summer home at Tadoussac and from her childhood until her death, Erie spent many summer months there each year.

When Willis died in 1887, Erie sold out her share of the family house in Tad (*Spruce Cliff*) and built a house opposite the Roman Catholic Church, called *Russellhurst*. In 1911 at age forty-eight, Erie married the widower, George de Guerry Languedoc who brought with him his daughter Adele. In his lifetime, George Languedoc was a civil engineer and architect, and for the first two years of their married life, they lived in Port Arthur, Ontario.

Subsequently, they moved to Ottawa where Erie remained until her husband's death in 1924 when she came to Montreal to live with her stepdaughter, Adele Languedoc, who was in charge of the McLennan Travelling Library at Macdonald College. She later sold *Russellhurst* in the Tadoussac village and bought what is now known as Languedoc Parc from the Dale family. She designed and built *Amberley* which is now (much renovated) the Gomer home. Dale also had a carriage road going down to Pointe Rouge. The circular "Fairy Circle" was its turnaround.

Erie Russell (Janes) Languedoc at Amberley

During World War I, Erie organized a Red Cross Society branch at Aylmer, Quebec, and after the war, she was instrumental in setting up seven chapters of the Imperial Order Daughters of the Empire (I.O.D.E., a Canadian national women's charitable organization) in the Ottawa district. In 1940, just before her death, Erie organized a Red Cross branch in Tadoussac. She was a life member of both the Red Cross Society and the I.O.D.E.

Erie did much to promote interest in, and the sale of, handicrafts indigenous to the Saguenay region and was an authority on the folklore of this district in Quebec.

Recognition of the work she had done for Tadoussac came with her election to the honorary presidency of Le Cercle des Fermieres of Tadoussac which still exists today.

Ann Stevenson Dewart relates memories of her first cousin, Erie.

"In those days the park was truly a private enclave, dominated by Cousin Erie Languedoc. No one passed her door without her scrutiny, and French and English alike walked in awe of her flashing, black eyes and outthrust jaw. 'You, there, what's your name?' she would ask, poking her crooked walking stick at the trespasser's stomach. If it was a French child, she would want to know his parents' names. She persuaded the Curé to declare the park off-limits after dark for the village youths, as much to protect her rest as their morals. Visitors were only allowed to come in by the front gate opposite the Golf Club. Tradesmen and the solitary motorcar had to use the back entrance near Hovington's farm. If anyone came to our door after dark, uninvited, Mum would first get down the .22 rifle before calling out, 'Who is it?' Fortunately, she never had to use either it or the revolver. Cousin Erie, however, wasn't afraid of man or beast and often stayed alone in the park until the boats stopped running late in September. She and her walking stick were a match for anything, but Mum was more nervous. Erie gave her a big brass dinner bell to ring if she needed help. Erie had one even bigger. As the only two women alone in the park it was a kind of mutual aid pact in case of fire or illness."

Erie died in 1941 when *Amberley* then went to Adele and later, after Adele's death, was acquired by Adelaide Gomer.

Nan & Lennox Williams

Caroline Anne (Nan) (Rhodes) Williams
1861-1937
& Bishop Lennox Williams, DD 1859-1958

Lennox Williams was born in 1859, in *Chapman House* at Bishop's College School located in Lennoxville, Quebec. His father, James Williams, was the fourth bishop of Quebec and he was born in Aberystwyth, Wales. His mother was Anna Maria Waldron, and she was born in 1821.

Lennox attended BCS as a boy and eventually became Head Prefect. He would often regale future generations of BCS family members with tales of experiences at the school and in particular his time as Head Prefect. Lennox studied theology at St. John's College, Oxford, and rowed for the college. His oar, with the names of the team members, still hangs on the wall of his cottage, *Brynhyfryd*, in Tadoussac.

Lennox was ordained in 1885 and began his career as curate at St Matthew's Church in Quebec. In 1899 he became the Dean of Quebec at Trinity Cathedral. In this role he would often travel in the summers to participate in confirmations throughout the eastern half of the province, including the Cote-Nord. In 1915 he was consecrated as the sixth bishop of Quebec and served until his retirement in 1935. Later in his life, he took services at the Protestant Chapel in Tadoussac.

Caroline Anne (Nan) Rhodes Williams was the seventh child of Col. William Rhodes and Anne Catherine Dunn. She was born in Sillery, Quebec in 1861. Her family called her "Annie" but to her children, she was known as "Nan". The ages of her brothers and sisters were spread over almost twenty years, yet they grew up actively engaged with each other. Armitage, her eldest brother, made her a big snow house; Godfrey took her and her sister Minnie skating and sliding. They all spent summers in Tadoussac together, Nan with her dog Tiney. She and her brother Godfrey frequently "apple-pied" all the beds, causing bedlam in the house. Growing up at *Benmore* the family home in Sillery, she was surrounded by an endless collection of birds and animals - geese, chickens, bantams, rabbits, guinea pigs, ducks and ponies, and even beehives. All were welcome inhabitants of her family's farm. Her brothers, Godfrey and Willy procured a bear cub and had a pole for it to climb. The family meals often included caribou and rabbit meat from her father's hunting trips. Croquet was a favourite family game on the lawn. In winter, Nan and her sister Minnie travelled by sleigh through the deep snow to their lessons at dancing school. Nan was a lively young girl who always loved jokes. Her father described her as "full of play".

Nan became engaged to Lennox when he was at St. Michael's Anglican Church in Sillery. She and Lennox Williams were married there in 1887. Her sister Gerty and her best friend Violet Montizambert were her bridesmaids. Their first child, James, was born in 1888, followed by Mary (Wallace) in 1890, Gertrude (Alexander) in 1894, and Sydney Williams in 1899.

As their children were growing up in Quebec, Lennox served at St. Michael's. His work always involved people and when he became Dean, and later Bishop of Quebec, his duties extended over the vast geography of the Quebec Diocese. Assisting him in his work brought Nan in contact with the many different people in the city and the province, some of whom would go overseas to serve in the South African (Boer) War, World War I, and World War II.

The winter of 1913-14 in Quebec was the last carefree time before World War I began. Nan always welcomed her children's friends around the Deanery for supper or tea. According to one of her future sons-in-law, "On some evenings it was quite amusing. The Dean and Mrs. Williams sat in his study, Jim Williams and Evelyn Meredith sat in an upstairs sitting room, Mary Williams and Jack Wallace in the drawing room, and Gertrude and Ronald Alexander in the dining room. Mrs. Williams was a very understanding person."

This was still the age of chaperones. Before going overseas, Jim and Evelyn were married, and both enjoyed summers in Tadoussac with the family at *Brynhyfryd*.

The war also brought devastation for the Williams family as it did for so many families of that generation. James, the eldest son, who had also attended Oxford University, was commissioned into the Canadian Army shortly after the war began. He served valiantly as an officer but was killed at the battle of the Somme in 1916. Lennox was devastated by the loss of his son and many said he was never the same after. Each summer Lennox would read the lesson about King David's son, Absalom, who was killed in battle and many of the congregation felt that Lennox was lamenting his own son's death.

It was in November 1916, that Nan received the news that her son Jim was killed, and two months later in January 1917, she and Lennox, accompanied by their daughters, Mary and Gertrude, sailed to England. Mary went to see Jack Wallace, Jim's best friend, and Gertrude was to be married to Ronald Alexander (who was serving with the Victoria Rifles). The wedding took place on February 19, 1917, with Mary participating as a bridesmaid. They stayed in London at Queen Anne's Mansions and remained there until April.

After the War, Nan and Lennox continued their active life together as Lennox had been consecrated as Bishop of Quebec in 1915. The Rhodes family house in Tadoussac, built in 1860, had been left to Nan.

It burnt down in 1932 and was rebuilt the next year. *Brynhyfryd* remains in Nan's family today. When Lennox retired in 1934, they had more time to spend in Tadoussac and ten grandchildren to enjoy it with them. One day, walking to town with one of her ten grandchildren, Nan discovered that her grandchild had lifted a bit of candy from Pierre Cid's General Store. She marched her back to return it and to apologize. To one of her grandchildren "Granny was always game for some fun and she had lots of energy." Nan loved to be out rowing the boats and like others her age, she swam regularly in the refreshing saltwater of the bay. On June 30, 1937, she climbed up the path from the beach and, reaching the house feeling a bit tired, she took a rest. Nan died suddenly later that evening.

Lennox's favourite book was *Alice in Wonderland*, which he would often quote to his grandchildren. His grandchildren also had many fond memories of their time with Lennox in Tadoussac. Every morning at eight the entire family would meet outside the dining room for prayers with everyone on their knees. Meals were served on time and exemplary manners were expected (elbows off the table). Afternoons were spent smoking his pipe or perhaps on special occasions a cigar, under the trees on the edge of the bank at *Brynhyfryd* with his white (Samoyed) dog Kara. Evenings were spent playing card games like Old Maid or Bridge with his children and grandchildren. He remained a great athlete and enjoyed tennis and golf into his old age. Eventually, in his nineties, he was slowed a little and transitioned from the golf course to the putting green at the hotel for his activity.

Lennox died in Tadoussac in his 100th year on the 8th of July 1958. The Lychgate at the Protestant Chapel in Tadoussac (roofed gateway at the entrance of the chapel) was donated by the congregation in his memory.

Mary Frances Russell Janes 1864-1915

Mary Frances Russell Janes' mother was born in Franklin, New Hampshire in 1836, the daughter of Willis Russell and Rebecca Page (Sanborn).

In 1843, when she was seven, Mary's family relocated to Quebec City where her father, Willis, entered the hotel business. In 1858, Mary married a Scotsman, William Duthie Baxter Janes and they moved to Montreal. Their first daughter, Mary Frances Russell Janes (1860) died within a week of her birth, and their second daughter, Elizabeth Anne Leavitte Janes (1861) died at the age of one. Erie Russell Janes (1863) was the third daughter. She survived and thrived, as did her younger sister who was given the same name as the first child, and is the subject of this biography, Mary Frances Russell Janes (1864).

In Willis Russell's biography, it was mentioned that a doctor recommended sea air for Willis's ailing daughter. His friend William Rhodes encouraged him to join him in Tadoussac, a plan that led to the construction of *Spruce Cliff* in 1861. It seems clear that Mary was that ailing daughter and sadly, tragedy struck one more time. In the days following this fourth daughter's birth, Willis's daughter, Mary, weakened and died in Quebec at the age of twenty-eight. She was buried in the family plot at Mount Hermon Cemetery in Quebec.

The two surviving children, Erie and Mary, went to live with their grandparents, Willis and Rebecca, who had built *Spruce Cliff* as a place for their daughter to heal. One can only hope that after being left with two babies and enduring three family deaths in five years, the cottage helped to heal the whole family.

Erie eventually married George de Guerry Languedoc and built *Amberley Cottage* in Languedoc Park. Mary never married and she continued to come to Tadoussac every summer to *Spruce Cliff*, staying with her grandparents until they died in the late 1880s, and then with her Uncle William and his three children. An old family letter reveals that she lived for a time with her sister, Erie, and her husband, George Languedoc, in Ottawa.

Mary died in 1915 at the age of fifty-one. In the chapel, both the baptismal font and a wall plaque are given in memory of her fifty years of summer residency in Tadoussac.

Henry Baring Powel 1864-1917

Henry was the youngest of Robert and Amy Powel's six children. He was born in Haddon, Camden, New Jersey in 1864. He married Edith Elizabeth Smith in 1888. She was the daughter of Robert Herbert Smith and Amelia Jane (LeMesurier) so this marriage connected the Powel and Smith families in Tadoussac. Henry and Edith had four children: Robert Hare 1888, Herbert De Veaux 1890, Harcourt 1896, and Blanche Valliere 1899.

His second son Herbert joined the Canadian Army and was killed in the Battle of Langemarck during World War I. His third son, Harcourt, called Harky, acquired *Fletcher Cottage* from his aunt, Blanche (Smith) Price and lived there in the summer up until he sold it to his first cousin's son, Bill Glassco.

Henry Baring passed away in 1917, in Chicoutimi.

Herbert Carington Smith 1866-1915

Herbert (Herbie) was born in Quebec City in 1866, the second son of Robert Herbert Smith and Amelia Jane LeMesurier.

He attended the Royal Military College in Kingston, Ontario. He had a long and distinguished army career. He served in the Dublin Fusiliers for twenty-seven years, receiving his commission in 1910. He was stationed in Egypt in 1898, under Lord Kitchener, also in South Africa (1899-1902) and Aden (1903). As a Lieutenant-Colonel he was serving as commanding officer of the 2nd Hampshire Regiment in the Dardanelles when he was shot and killed during World War I at the Battle of Gallipoli, Turkey on April 25, 1915. He is buried at the Helles Memorial at the tip of the Gallipoli Peninsula, Turkey.

He was survived by his wife Helen (Lawton) and a daughter, Helen Carington 1910-1932.

Howard Henry Ransom 1867-1925

Howard Henry Ransom was born in Montreal in 1867. His parents, Howard Ransom and Maria Benallack were both from Montreal. He is listed as having been a merchant in Montreal and in 1890 Howard Henry married Jane Parslow who died without having had any children.

In 1896 Howard married Isabella Linley, who had been born in 1866, the daughter of Charles Linley and Isabella Jones. They had two children, Howard Charles Linley Ransom (1903-1976), and Audrey Isabel Gertrude (Scadding) Ransom (1904 -1992).

The family lived in Hochelaga for about twenty years but later moved to Westmount, Quebec. Howard served on the Westmount City Board of Assessors for seventeen years and became its chairman. He was a member of St. Mathias Church, was greatly interested in the Anglican Church, and for many years was lay secretary of the Synod of Montreal, taking an active part in deliberations.

Howard became ill and died on May 10, 1925, at age fifty-eight. He was survived by his wife, Isabelle Linley, his son, Charles, and daughter, Audrey Scadding. Howard Ransom is buried in Montreal. Isabella died on October 19th, 1945, in Westmount, and is also buried in Montreal.

Charles Carington Smith 1867-1952
& Aileen (Dawson) Smith 1874-1959

Charles was the third son of Robert Harcourt Smith and Amelia Jane (LeMesurier) of Quebec City. He was educated at Upper Canada College. His banking career began with the Toronto branch of the Quebec Bank. He won many awards in the 1890s for rowing and canoeing.

In the early 1900s, he moved to Quebec, continuing his career with the Quebec Bank, and was a member of the Quebec Bank hockey team that won the bank hockey championships in Montreal in 1900.

In 1901 Charles married Aileen Dawson. Aileen was the daughter of Col. George Dudley Dawson and his wife of County Carlow, Ireland, and was born in Toronto. Charles and Aileen had four children: Doris Amelia (1902), George Noel (1904), Herbert, (1906), and May (1908). Their daughter Doris married Jack Molson and their Molson descendants continue to summer in Tadoussac.

The family moved to Montmorency Falls where they lived for the rest of Charles's working career, which continued with the Royal Bank of Canada after their take-over of the Quebec Bank in 1917.

They retired to Kingston, Ontario from where annual summer visits to Tadoussac were much enjoyed.

Sir William and Lady Price

Sir William Price 1867-1924 & Amelia Blanche Carrington (Smith) 1863-1947

William Price was born in Talca Chile to Henry Ferrier Price 1833-1898 and Florence Stoker Rogerson. He was the eldest of seven children, two of whom died in infancy. His surviving siblings were Henry Edward (Harry), Arthur John, Terracita (Terry), and Florence (Flo).

Amelia Blanche Carrington Smith was born in Quebec City to Robert Herbert Carrington Smith 1825-1898 and Amelia Jane LeMesurier 1832-1917. She had six brothers and one sister.

The three original 'Price Brothers' of what would become the Price Brothers Pulp and Paper Company were William Evan, Evan John, and David Edward. All three were bachelors. Having no legitimate heir, they persuaded their brother Henry Ferrier and his family, then living in Chile, to return to Canada. Their eldest son, William, arrived in Canada in 1879. After one semester at Bishop's College School, he was sent to St Mark's in England where he completed his studies in 1886 and started his apprenticeship with Price Brothers. In 1899, with the death of the last surviving 'Price Brother', he became sole proprietor, president and managing director of the family business. William inherited a tottering empire, heavily indebted, technically in receivership -- more one of potential than actual wealth. In the first decade of the 20th century, William planned and built a large newsprint mill in the town of Kenogami. The Kenogami Mill, the most productive newsprint mill in the world at that time, began operations in 1912. William associated with James Buchanan Duke, the legendary North Carolina tobacco tycoon and Max Aitken (Lord Beaverbrook),helped with financing for the Kenogami Mill and the development of hydroelectric power with the Ille Maligne Dam and Power Plant in which he and Duke were partners.

In 1884 William married Amelia Blanche Smith at the Cathedral of the Holy Trinity in Quebec City. Three years his senior and a celebrated beauty, she would bear him eight children. The surviving six were John (Jack), Arthur

Sir William Price at Anse St Jean in 1923

Clifford (Coosie), Charles Edward, Willa (Glassco), Richard Harcourt (Dick) and Jean (Harvey).

On August 7, 1914, William was asked, by the minister of the Militia, to build, in twenty days, a camp where troops could be assembled and trained. William shut down his establishments, moved his workforce to Valcartier, and built the camp on schedule. Quebec had been selected as the port of embarkation for the Canadian Expeditionary Force and William was appointed Director General of Embarkation. William was not a soldier. He had, however, joined Quebec's militia 8th Royal Rifles and risen to Captain when he resigned in 1903.

For his contribution to the War effort, William was knighted by King George V on January 1, 1915.

On October 2nd, 1924, Sir William was taken down by a landslide on the Au Sable River behind the Kenogami Mill. His body was found ten days later in the Saguenay River at St. Fulgence. His grave lies at the end of Price Park in Kenogami on the point of a high cliff overlooking the confluence of the Au Sable and Saguenay Rivers where he lost his life. He would be pleased that the focus of the Sir William Price Museum in Kenogami is on the employees of the Company. He deeply appreciated their loyalty and work skills and touched their lives in ways their descendants remember fondly to this day.

Sir William was foremost a family man, a patriot, an industrial visionary and a builder; amongst them, it is difficult to say which stood first. His wife did not share his fascination for a remote, largely wilderness area and his love of the outdoors and rarely came to the Saguenay/Lac St-Jean region. Nevertheless, he was a loving and inspirational father and nobody who knew him mentioned his name without talking of his affection for children.

Along with his business, war efforts, political activities and sports William was President of the Quebec Harbour Commission in 1912 and Director of many companies including Union Bank, the Canadian General Electric Company, the Wayagamack Pulp and Paper Company Ltd., The Montreal Trust Company, The Quebec Railway, Light and Power Co., The Transcontinental Railway and the Prudential Trust Company.

William's first mention of Tadoussac is in a letter written during the summer of 1880 to his parents who were still in Chile. He tells of happy days spent in a canoe in the bay fishing for Tommy cod, perhaps hinting at the renowned salmon fisherman he would become. He did not spend much time in Tadoussac but he did acquire *Fletcher Cottage*, a lifelong source of pleasure for his wife. He also bought the *Pilot House* and the *Harry Price House*, which he gave to Harry for his family and as a place for their sister Terry to spend her summers.

After Sir William's untimely death Blanche moved from 145 Grande Allee to Ave de Bernier in Quebec City where she lived until her death in 1947. She was fortunate in her companion, Muriel Hudsbeth, daughter of Dean Evans and his first wife.

We are told Blanche was handsome and charming and though her memory faded her charm did not. During summers in *Fletcher Cottage*, her sister Edith (Edie) and brother Edmond were with her. Also in residence for the summer were many grandchildren - ten or more at times. By then she remembered only 'long ago stories' yet continued to extend a warm welcome and to look most elegant, dressed in black as she had since the death of her husband.

She is buried in Mount Hermon Cemetery in Quebec City.

Louisa Jane Burns d. 1921

There is a plaque dedicated to the memory of Louisa Jane Burns but all it tells us is that she died on August 4th, 1921, and that it was installed by her nieces and/or nephews. More information has not been found in spite of many attempts and inquiries, which serves to illustrate the purpose of this book.

Henry Edward Price 1869-1954
& Helen Muriel (Gilmour) 1879-1952

Henry Edward (Harry) Price was born in Zemita, Chile in 1869, the second son out of seven children of Henry Ferrier Price and Florence Stoker Rogerson.

As with all his brothers and sisters, he was baptized in the Roman Catholic Church and had Roman Catholics stand proxy for their godparents. Little else is known about their childhood in Chile. At the age of eleven in 1880, he and his older brother William were sent from Chile to Wolfesfield in Sillery, Quebec. There they were to live with their uncles and aunts so they could be educated to take over the company, as none of the three Price Brothers and their sisters then living at Wolfesfield was married or had children. At the time the two boys arrived in Canada, they only spoke Spanish. As the aunts and uncles forbade them to speak Spanish to one another, they learned English in a hurry. From the stories Henry told his children, they were quite lonely.

Henry attended Trinity College School, Port Hope from 1884 to 1888. After leaving TCS, he lived with his parents (who by then had moved to Canada from Chile) while attending Osgoode Hall Law School from which he graduated. Afterwards, he articled at the firm of Blake, Lash and Cassels, in Toronto. During the mid to late 1890s, he moved to Quebec City to become corporate legal counsel for Price Brothers and following the death of their uncle Evan John in 1899, his brother William became President of Price Brothers.

Helen Muriel Gilmour was born in Quebec City in 1879 as the first child of John David Gilmour and Helen Shamberg Fraser. She was usually known as Mimi or Muriel and had two brothers Kenneth and Dudley born in 1881 and 1882 respectively.

Her family had founded Allan Gilmour and Co. in Quebec in the 1820s. Muriel was the granddaughter of John Gilmour, a contemporary of the first William Price who arrived in Quebec in 1810 and was an equally renowned lumber merchant. Her mother, Helen Fraser, came from Port Hope in Ontario and was related to the Wotherspoon and Cumberland families. Much of Muriel's childhood was spent in Port

Hope, her mother's hometown, where she was educated.

Harry married Helen Muriel Gilmour in 1901 at St. Andrew's Church in Quebec. He had to ask her three times to marry him before she finally accepted. All of their ten children, starting with Helen Florence, were born in Quebec between 1902 and 1921. Their youngest daughter, Joan, died of diphtheria or scarlet fever in 1924.

Harry was instrumental in founding the Quebec Golf Club, one of North America's oldest. In 1915, it was compelled to move out of the Plains of Abraham and east to its present-day location near Montmorency Falls. In 1934, King George V granted it the privilege to add the "Royal" prefix to its name. In the winter Harry was a keen curler.

They lived at 2 St. Denis Ave, 16 St. Denis Ave., and 269 Laurier Ave. At the time they were comfortably off, as their daughter Helen spoke of trips to Europe in 1913, 1921 and 1928. The wedding of her sister Enid to Sydney Williams at the Cathedral of the Holy Trinity in 1929 was a grand occasion.

In the early 1920s, they were given the use of the house *Casa Nueva* (also known as the *Harry Price House*) in Tadoussac by Sir William Price after Harry and William's mother, Florence Rogerson Price died. The only condition was understood to be that when their sister Terry was in Tadoussac she would stay at *Casa Nueva* and not next door at *Fletcher Cottage*.

Harry was the Corporate Secretary of Price Brothers until the time of the depression when they lost their money with the bankruptcy of Price Brothers in 1933 because of their stockbroker's inability (or deliberate decision not) to sell all their investments when requested. During the depression, they had to take in boarders, but they never let their old Nanny go. She stayed with them until they both died when she went to live with Ida Price. Helen stayed with them for quite a while, as did Milly until she went off to Europe to join the war effort in 1941. Jimmy also remained with them until both his parents died. In 1948 they gave Jimmy the family house in Tadoussac in appreciation for all he had done for his parents.

As a result of the financial difficulties, Muriel set up an investment account for all her children and grandchildren, which was managed by her son Jimmy, a stockbroker. This account continued throughout the lives of her children until 2008.

During the 1940s tragedy unrelated to the war struck as three of their children died within five years. First Gilly was killed in an industrial accident at the Price Brothers mill in Riverbend in 1940. Evan was killed in an airplane accident in 1944, on his way to a funeral for a family friend. That same year Iso died in Ottawa after a long illness. During the war when their fathers were away in Europe, Harry visited all his Williams and Smith grandchildren every night to wish them good night.

Many of their grandchildren remember Harry and Muriel in Tadoussac in the years after the war. Stories abound of Harry buying ice cream cones for his grandchildren on Cartier Avenue in Quebec or right before their lunch in Tadoussac. He also cheated while endlessly playing patience. They remember Muriel in Tadoussac for giving herself her daily needles for her diabetes after boiling them and yelling at Harry who was ten years older to tell him what he was supposed to be doing next. Some of their grandchildren lived with them while finishing the grade twelve high school courses they needed to qualify for post-secondary education. They celebrated their fiftieth wedding anniversary in November 1951.

Helen Muriel died in Quebec in 1952, when she suddenly collapsed on the way to bed with only her deaf husband in the house at the time. Help arrived shortly afterwards, however, when her son Jimmy arrived home. Henry Edward died at the Jeffrey Hale Hospital in Quebec in 1954.

George Carington Smith 1870-1946

George (Tommy) Carington Smith was born in Quebec City in 1870. He was the fourth son of Robert Herbert Smith and Amelia Jane LeMesurier. He was a banker and spent most of his career with the Bank of Montreal. He married Winifred Dawes in 1899 in Lachine, Quebec.

They had three children. His son, David Norman, died in infancy. His daughter, Winifred Noeline (known as Pixie), was born in 1902 and his daughter, Marion Sarah Smith Dobson, was born in 1907. He died in 1946 in Montreal and is buried in the Mount Royal Cemetery in Montreal.

May Dawson 1870-1967

The Dawson family was one of the earliest supporters and summer attendees of the Tadoussac Protestant Chapel. The first of four children born to George Dudley Dawson and Elizabeth Crooks, May Dawson had a cognitive disability that required her to have caregivers with her at all times. It is remarkable that in a day and age when most families facing this kind of challenge had their affected children committed to institutions, the Dawsons kept her with them at home.

George Dudley Dawson, May's father, was a wine merchant descended from an Anglican Irish family. May's mother, Elizabeth Crooks, was from a third-generation Upper Canadian family with roots in Scotland. While May remained single, her younger siblings Aileen, Richard, and Dudley Dawson all married. Different members of the family, particularly Aileen, took turns caring for her.

Aileen married Charles Carington Smith, and they had three children the youngest of whom they also named May. The oldest was Doris Carington Smith who later married Jack Molson. To Doris and her two younger siblings, May Dawson was always simply "Auntie May". After Doris married C.J.G. "Jack" Molson, "Auntie May" would often stay with them here in Tadoussac.

May was fond of sewing and other handicrafts. She was remembered with much affection by those who knew her.

Edmund Harcourt Carington Smith 1874-1951

Edmund was born in Quebec City in 1874. He was the fifth son of Robert Herbert Smith and Amelia Jane LeMesurier Smith.

He was a well-known banking figure who started his career at the Bank of Montreal in 1892. He was manager of several branches in Canada and England and ended his career in 1932 in charge of the Charlevoix and Centre Street branches of the bank in Quebec City. He was a member for many years of the Royal Montreal Curling Club and the Montreal Athletic Amateur Association.

He spent many summers in Tadoussac and loved the beauty of the area and, as a bachelor, he enjoyed the closeness of his extended family. He died suddenly in Tadoussac on August 15, 1951, and is buried at Mount Hermon Cemetery in Quebec City.

Arthur Carington Smith 1875-1952

Arthur was born in Quebec City in 1875, the sixth son of Robert Herbert Smith and Amelia Jane LeMesurier. His older brothers were Robert, Herbert, Charles, George, and Edmund. He also had two sisters, Edith and Blanche. He attended the Royal Military College in Kingston.

He married Constance Naomi Hamilton also of Quebec City. They had one son, Hugh Hamilton 1909-1974.

Arthur played hockey for the Quebec Bulldogs and was a prolific goal scorer. He was influential in the introduction of netting between the goalposts to ensure the confirmation of goals scored!

He served overseas in the First World War with the Royal Rifles.

Arthur was a banker but ended up his career as a stockbroker for Greenshields in Quebec City.

As with all the Smith boys, his true love was Tadoussac and his boat the *Empress of Tadoussac*. He was the favourite uncle to a large number of Smith and Price offspring. To be invited to sail with Uncle Art was the highlight of the summer. The stories of the adventures on the Empress are legends.

Uncle Art with the Empress of Tadoussac

Nonie Stevenson, Mabel Russell & Grace Scott just off the (CSL!) boat

Mabel Emily (Russell) Scott 1875-1952
& Charles Cunningham Scott 1876-1955

Mabel Emily Russell was the granddaughter of Willis Russell and the daughter of William Edward Russell and Fanny Eliza Pope. Her sister was Florence Louisa "Nonie" Russell and her brother was Willis Robert Russell who died at age twenty of tuberculosis.

Mabel was born in Quebec City and married Charles Cunningham Scott, also from Quebec, at age twenty-seven. Charles was a sergeant in the 8th Royal Rifles in Quebec City. He fought in the Boer War with the Royal Canadian Regiment from 1899-1900. After the war, he worked for the Quebec/Lac St. Jean Railway until 1914.

Mabel and Charles relocated to Buffalo, New York, where Charles continued his career as sales manager for a steam equipment company called Worthington Pump & Machinery.

They had two children, Frances Grace Scott and Charles Russell Scott. Mabel and Charles and their children continued summering in Tadoussac at the family cottage, *Spruce Cliff*. Charles also loved to take

Russell fishing in the Kawartha Lakes.

Mabel died near Buffalo at age seventy-six in 1952 and her husband, Charles, died a few years later, in 1955.

Their daughter, Frances Grace Scott, never married and became a schoolteacher in the Buffalo area (Kenmore) where she lived until her death in 1993 at age eighty-eight. Grace's brother, Russell, married Christine Marchington. Both Russ and Grace continued summering at Tadoussac at *Spruce Cliff* throughout their lives.

Russell died in London, Ontario in 1995, and his wife, Christine, died in 2010. Their two children are Susan and Robert Scott who both summered in Tadoussac as children. Susan (Susie) married George Bruemmer and they, along with children Andrew, Matthew, and Jennifer, continue enjoying some or all of their summers in *Spruce Cliff Cottage*, with the occasional visit from brother Bob.

Frederick Courtnay Price 1877-1898 & Llewellyn Price 1878-1899

Frederick and Llewellyn were the youngest sons of Henry Ferrier Price and Florence Rogerson Price. They were both born in Chile while the family was living there; Frederick in 1877 and Llewellyn in 1878. Their older siblings were Sir William, Henry Edward, Teresa Jane, Arthur John and Florence Mary (Bradshaw).

After the family returned to Canada in 1884, they lived in Toronto and both Frederick and Llewellyn attended Ridley College in St. Catherine's, Ontario.

Sadly, both brothers died at age twenty-one. Frederick died in Toronto in 1898 of tuberculosis and is buried in Mt. Pleasant Cemetery. Llewellyn died in 1999 of diphtheria and is buried in the family plot at Mount Hermon Cemetery, Sillery, Quebec.

Dr Stevenson on Adele's Beach with his three daughters, Elizabeth, Ann and Margaret

Florence Louisa Maude "Nonie" (Russell) 1877-1940 & Dr. James Stevenson 1878-1957

Florence Louisa Maude Russell was born in Quebec in 1877, the daughter of William Edward Russell and Fanny Eliza (Pope) and granddaughter of Willis Russell. When she was sixteen, she went to Montreal, ostensibly to visit Trevor Evans's family (he was an old beau from Tadoussac days) but instead falsified her age and enrolled as a student nurse at the Montreal General Hospital.

By her own admission, her course marks were never very good, but she was tops when it came to working on the wards. Tall, strong, and energetic, she did twelve-hour shifts and often twenty-four. It was while she was at the M.G.H. that she met her future husband, James Stevenson, who was at McGill University studying medicine. Upon graduation, she returned to Quebec as Night Supervisor at the Jeffrey Hale Hospital, and James Stevenson followed her there as Surgical Resident. They married in the summer of 1905.

Ann Stevenson described her parents in her book *Nose to the Window*, excerpts from which appear below.

"Dr. Stevenson was born in Montreal in February 1878, the youngest son of Pillans Scarth Stevenson and Annie Story Harris. The Stevensons had come out from Leith, Scotland, where they were ship owners, settling near Ottawa after the Napoleonic wars.

They were a large family but we have lost touch with all except the Scarth connection. Dad's mother was a Harris from a Boston family who had married into the LeBrun de Duplessis-Charles family and settled in Montreal.

Mum was a completely uninhibited person, especially for a Victorian woman. Her father had taught them all that it was far better to talk about a thing or do it than to keep it inside and stew about it. She loved laughter, bright lights, sweet music, fine furniture and silver, and good food. Reading, other than light novels, was beyond her interest, nor did she do any handiwork or sewing, having lost the sight of one eye during pregnancy, although as a girl she had shown considerable talent with oils.

When she hated, she hated with every fibre of her being. When she loved, it was total. There were no half-measures in anything she did. If a project didn't turn out, she kept at it until it did. In spite of her love of life, she was subject to frequent bouts of depression. Dark days depressed her, death frightened her, and thunderstorms terrified her. Then she would pace the floor wringing her hands and shrieking at every bolt. (The house at Tadoussac had been struck when she was a child, and she had been knocked unconscious).

She attended church at the Cathedral quite regularly until she took issue with the Dean over a sermon he preached on the text, 'Think well of thyself,' and we all transferred to St. Matthew's. She didn't return to the Cathedral until the Dean moved on up the line and became Bishop somewhere. Her Anglicanism didn't prevent her from having a few miraculous medals or making offerings to St. Anthony to help her find lost trinkets.

Compassion was her religion. We were taught to pick flowers and take them to the old people at *St. Bridget's Home* across the street, as we, too, might be old and lonely someday. As a child, I would be sent on the streetcar to take a hot casserole to a destitute widow. Unfortunately, I was also sent on the same streetcar to bring home a bottle of straight alcohol which she kept hidden in her bureau drawer and imbibed secretly at bedtime. (This was before the days of sleeping pills and tranquillizers.) It was also my task to dispose of the empties over the fence of the nearest vacant lot. During this time, she was very unhappy, and she and Dad fought bitterly until the small hours of the morning. Everything Dad did annoyed her, and she didn't hesitate to tell him so. He, in turn, retreated more and more into his books. It was an unhappy time for all of us.

Mum was a fabulous cook and fed anyone and everyone who came in her door. She fought a continuous, losing battle with her weight because she had to sample everything to see if it was up to standard. She would hold a piece of cake to her ear and press it lightly to "hear if it had enough eggs in it." Crusty bread, rich cakes, suet puddings, sucre à la crème, and huge roasts issued from the kitchen with joyous profusion, to be devoured by our boyfriends, who enjoyed her company as much as ours. Because of her weight problem, she walked miles each day in all weather and for a while took up curling when walking in the winter was too difficult.

In later years Mum's health began to deteriorate. The long hours on her feet, cooking, walking, and working collapsed her arches and she suffered from prolonged and frequent bouts of phlebitis and varicose veins, and probably arthritis. Her heart, worn out by work and the intensity of her emotions, began to fibrillate, and for three years she was too weak to leave her bed. Late in January 1940, I arrived unexpectedly in Quebec to visit her in the hospital. Though no one had told her I was coming, she said to the nurse, 'Is Ann here yet? Will Elizabeth get here in time?' They thought her mind was wandering, as it so often had during her illness. Somehow, she who had seen so many people die, knew when her own time had come. She died that night.

Dr James Stevenson remained at the Jeffrey Hale Hospital where he was the head surgeon. Although he had great compassion for the widows and the needy, he showed it in very practical ways. When he suspected that little Leontyne Déschênes at Tadoussac had tuberculosis of the hip, he took her out of the hands of the local 'ramancheur' (bonesetter) and brought her to Québec for six months of free hospitalization and care. If a person was poor,

The Three Stevenson Sisters, Ann, Elizabeth and Margaret

he never charged a cent. However, he made it up by charging the wealthy patients whatever the traffic would bear. He held free clinics on his weekends at Tadoussac, doing minor treatments on his front gallery. He was a skilful surgeon and a charter fellow of the Royal College of Surgeons (Canada)."

'Nonie' Russell and Dr. Stevenson had three daughters, all of whom married and eventually had their own cottages in Languedoc Park on land given to them by their cousin, Erie Russell (Janes) Languedoc. Margaret Stevenson married John Reilley, Elizabeth Stevenson married Lionel O'Neill, and Ann Stevenson married the Rev. Russell Dewart.

'Nonie' died in Quebec in 1940 and Dr. Stevenson died in Montreal in 1957.

Trevor Ainslie Evans 1879-1939 & Dorothy Gwendolyn Esther (Rhodes) 1892-1977

Trevor Ainslie Evans was born in Montreal in 1879, the son of the Very Reverend Thomas Lewis Frye Evans, Dean of Montreal, and Maye Stewart Bethune. He married Dorothy Gwendolyn Esther Rhodes, the eldest daughter of Armitage Rhodes in Quebec City after World War I.

As a boy, Trevor spent the summers in Tadoussac as his father conducted Sunday services at the Tadoussac Protestant Chapel. He stayed in the house currently owned by the Beattie family. Trevor attended the High School of Montreal located on University Street and he initially served with the Royal Victoria Rifles which, at the beginning of World War I, amalgamated with several other Companies and Militia Regiments as the First Royal Montreal Regiment. He went overseas and saw action at the Somme where he was twice wounded. Trevor recovered from his injuries at 'Broadlands' in England an estate owned by his aunt and uncle, Edward and Stretta Price.

Dorothy Rhodes was born in 1892, in Quebec City. Dorothy was the daughter of Armitage Rhodes of *Benmore*, Bergerville in Quebec City and Phoebe Allman. Dorothy spent her summers in Tadoussac with her family. She was 'home schooled' and then attended local schools before going to Miss Porter's School in Farmington, Connecticut, and then King's Hall in Compton, Quebec.

Dorothy served with the Canadian Expeditionary Force as a nursing sister during World War I.

In 1921 Dorothy and Trevor purchased *Ivanhoe* from the Royal Trust Company and the executors of the Estate of the late Alfred Piddington of Quebec City.

Trevor established an insurance agency for the North American Insurance Company on St. Sacrement Street in Old Montreal. He was a member of the St. James's Club in a building that was demolished to make way for the building of Place Ville Marie.

During his summers in Tadoussac, he played golf (left-handed) with his hickory shafted golf clubs. He regularly fished the last hour of the rising tide and the first hour of the falling tide. He also dabbled in

Dorothy and Trevor Evans with daughters Phoebe and Ainslie

watercolour painting and in writing poetry. Their children, born between 1921 and 1925, were Phoebe Maye (Evans) Skutezky, Dorothy Ainslie (Evans) Stephen, Trevor Lewis Armitage Evans, and Rhodes Bethune (Tim) Evans.

During her summers Dorothy managed her children and their many friends. When they had their own families, she welcomed her grandchildren and presented them with a list of chores and responsibilities. It was not uncommon for there to be twenty people for dinner.

Frank and Carrie Morewood at Windward

Caroline Annie (Rhodes) 1881-1973
& Francis Edmund Morewood 1886-1949

Carrie was born in 1881, to William Rhodes and Caroline Annie Hibler in Adelaide, Australia. William was superintendent of railway systems and was presumably in Australia to assist in building their railway. Carrie's first visit to Tadoussac was in the summer of 1882. When in Tadoussac the family stayed at the original Rhodes cottage that was on the same site as today's *Brynhyfryd*. In 1885-86 Carrie and her mother again visited Australia. A brother Godfrey was born in 1890 and died in 1892. The family lived in Philadelphia but spent much of their time at Benmore in Quebec City, especially when William was travelling.

William's sister, Minnie, married Harry Morewood. The family lived in New York but spent a great deal of time at *Benmore* and Tadoussac –

important because one of their sons, Frank, born 1886, would eventually marry Carrie in 1919 or 1920. Carrie was thirty-eight when she married, Frank about thirty-five, and they had two children, Bill and Betty.

Nothing is known about Carrie's schooling, but Frank went to Bishop's College School in Lennoxville at age fourteen. It is believed that Frank was an architect and he designed several houses in Tadoussac: *Windward*, the Turcot house, and the new *Brynhyfryd*. He also did a great deal of design work for the chapel, having the steps and the back door added to the building in cement, as well as the rose window on the street side.

Frank was said to have had polio; Betty Evans, his daughter, told stories of how he had to manually lift his left leg to step on the brake while driving, which made for a terrifying trip from Quebec City to Tadoussac on the old, narrow, and hilly roads. Frank was an artist and many of his watercolours are hanging in houses in Tadoussac. He died in 1949, having met just one of his grandchildren, Anne Evans, whose only memory of him is having him paint her face like a bunny.

After Frank's death, Carrie lived with their son Bill and his family outside Philadephia. She travelled often to Lennoxville and Tadoussac to spend time with their daughter Betty Evans and her family. Carrie was active in the church in Pennsylvania. She was a quiet, gentle woman who did not interfere with the upbringing of her grandchildren but had a big influence on all of them. She was a very positive role model. Granddaughter Anne remembers her catching her doing something she was forbidden to do in Tadoussac, and telling her she would not tell her parents if she promised never to do it again. Somehow when Granny gave a reason why it was dangerous it made sense, so Anne did not do it again.

As an old lady Carrie (Granny) had some sort of palsy so she typed everything. When Anne was first married, Granny wrote to her every week and Anne wrote back every Friday while sitting at the laundromat. When Anne and Ian Belton bought their first house, she gave them a washer and dryer! Uncle Bill told Anne that Granny fussed terribly if her note did not arrive on Wednesday.

She had a series of heart attacks in her last few years and died in

Morewood, Catherine Rhodes and Frank Morewood rowing on the Saguenay

1973. At that time, she had met her first great-grandchild and knew the second was on the way and would be named Carrie, after her. And today, Carrie (Belton) Mintz and her older brother Ian Belton love to come and stay in their great-grandmother's house with their own families.

Willis Robert Russell 1887-1907

Willis Robert Russell was the son of William Edward Russell and Fanny Eliza Pope. He was the brother of Florence Louisa "Nonie" Russell and Mabel Emily Russell. We don't know anything else about Willis Robert other than that he died in Quebec at age twenty from tuberculosis.

Marjorie (Webb) Turcot 1887-1976

Marjorie's sisters were Dorothy, who married Arthur Warburton, and Rachel who married Dennis Stairs and summered next door to Marjorie in what is now the Durnford's cottage.

Marjorie (Webb) and her husband Percival Turcot were the parents of four children, John (1920), Elliott (1922), Peter (1925), and Joan, (1928). The two who shared the cottage in Tadoussac were John and his wife Marjorie, and their children Cheryl, John, David and Greg, and Peter and Anne, and their children Wendy, Peggy, Peter, Chris, and Susan.

Marjorie Webb grew up on St. Denis Street in Quebec City. As a nurse she served overseas from 1914 to 1919, spending significant time on the front lines at the Casualty Clearing Stations in France for which she was decorated with the Royal Red Cross. In a letter home to her mother, she wrote: "I am sorry I have not been telling you about the work, it's rather hard to write about. Lately, since the tents were opened, we have been getting all the stretcher cases. The wounds are pretty hard to look at but you get used to it." She was stationed at the front including spending time at the horrific Battle of the Somme.

Percy Turcot grew up in Quebec City and vacationed with his family in St. Irenée. He also served on the front lines in World War I as a Captain and was wounded. He went on to a career as a shipping executive with Mclean Kennedy, a shipping broker. In 1916, shortly after being commissioned to France from England, he wrote to Marjorie: "It is a great feeling to at last feel you are going to try to do something. There is no truer saying than – 'The only man who is happy today is the man at the front.'" Even at the age of thirty, he needed permission from his mother as he was the sole supporter of his family. "I had a hard time getting my mother's permission, but she said yes yesterday, I am now in for it. I was very hard on poor mother."

They were married in 1919 shortly after Marjorie returned from Europe. All four children were born in St. John, New Brunswick before moving to Montreal around 1930.

Marjorie and Percy purchased their Tadoussac property from Rachel Stairs and built the existing Turcot house in 1946. Marjorie and her son Peter, aged twenty-one, spent the summer in Tad overseeing the construction and building the path to the beach, while Percy working in the shipping business made sure that post-war supplies were delivered.

Teatime was a ritual with friends in the afternoon in the front yard in Tadoussac, and every Sunday in Westmount, with lots and lots of family. Grandchildren were given free run of the house on Belmont Avenue, which included playing super eight family movies, ping pong games, and watching Walt Disney. The house in Tad was often overflowing with guests and family.

Marjorie was a prolific reader who loved picnics, berry picking, and flowers. Percy was an avid sportsman. Rumour has it he would play nine holes of golf before work in St John, NB every day. Both played tennis, and golf, and skied, but not on Sunday.

They were opposites in so many ways and yet married for fifty-seven years. Marjorie, a devoted Anglican, was serious and generous to

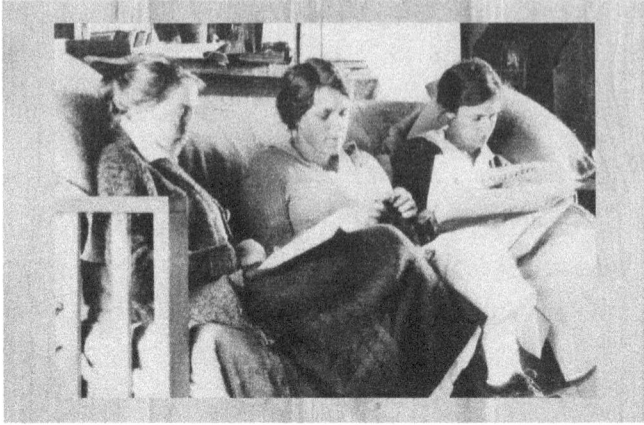

Rachel (Webb) Stairs, Gertrude (Williams) Alexander & Dorothy (Rhodes) Evans in Brynhyfryd. They went to King's Hall, Compton together resulting in the Webb sisters coming to Tadoussac!

a fault with a keen interest in everyone she met and interacted with. Percy attended the Catholic Church and was a true Quebecer who lived his life full of "joie de vivre" ... however one common trait was you were always warmly welcomed by both into their home. "Last touch" by Gammie's cane was always a game with the grandchildren on the way out the door.

Betty Evans made the needlepoint seat cushion for one of the chairs at the front of the church in Tad in memory of Marjorie Turcot and the carved wooden top on the font at the back of the church was also given in her memory (carved by Pierre Tremblay).

Percy, having a career in the shipping business, would raise shipping flags with the help of his grandchildren, to salute the passing Headline ships on the Saguenay to see if they would toot their horn in response, which they did on occasion. The funnel colours for the Headline ships were black bearing the 'Red Hand of Ulster' with three drops of blood on a white shield. The bloody hand became a theme of many ghost stories told at Tad bonfires on the beach.

Marjorie was one of the first women to vote in Canada. In 1917 The federal government granted limited war-time suffrage to enlisted women in 1917 (*Military Voters Act*, awarded the vote to women serving in the armed forces as well as nurses in the war) and was followed by full suffrage for women in 1918.

Lily Bell Rhodes 1889-1975

"Quick! Get a jar. Let's take it to Lily Bell!"

With those words, an oddly attractive, but rare insect would (to its astonishment) find itself trapped behind glass and on its way to being sketched by Lily Bell, an avid artist and lover of all things natural. And whatever that bug looked like she would gently turn it loose in a safe corner of the yard when she was done.

The daughter of Francis Rhodes (fourth son of Col. Rhodes and Anne Dunn) and Totie LeMoine, she would likely have been brought up in the LeMoine family home, known as *Spencer Grange*, in Quebec City, which became the Lieutenant-Governor's residence, and then a Canadian Heritage property and museum.

Lily Bell had a sister Frances and two other sisters who died in infancy. One of those, Anne, died before Lily Bell was born but the other, Gertrude, was born when she was seven years old. She was distraught when that child died, and whether that contributed to her nervousness as a young girl can only be speculated upon. Neither Frances nor Lily Bell ever married.

Lily Bell was always very good at sketching and devoted a great deal of her time to developing her artistic skills. Her maternal grandfather was the Canadian author, historian, and past President of The Royal Society of Canada, Sir James McPherson Le Moine (1825-1912).

Lily Bell studied art at Les Ecoles des Beaux-Arts in Quebec City under Henry Ivan Neilson (Professor of Painting, Drawing, and Anatomy), as well as with instructor and noted Canadian artist Jean-Paul Lemieux. It was said: "Although Miss Rhodes painted for her own enjoyment and is not a listed artist, her competency of composition, perspective, and palette … underscores an undeniable and elevated degree of ability."

But in Tadoussac, she was remembered for being very soft-spoken and sweet. She adored children and would take her young nieces on walks in the woods, telling them the names of all the flowers and mushrooms they could find, and firing their imaginations by insisting there were fairies dancing under each of them. Not surprisingly she was a great gardener along with her sister, Frances, and loved animals, particularly dogs which she used to sketch often. She even had a favourite white sweater made from the fur of a long-haired dachshund she used to own. She would frequently be seen sitting very still on a log or rock under a shapeless sunhat quietly sketching some composition that had caught her eye. Many of these sketches became very small paintings that were given to her many cousins in Tadoussac.

In the summers she usually stayed with her cousin, Lennox Williams, for a week or so, and then after he died, she was made welcome in the home of her friend, Grace Scott.

Looking back now, one can only imagine there was a depth to her that few of us knew. What we remember is her loving kindness and her reverence for nature. And some of us are still trying to collect her delightful paintings when they come available.

Violet Mary (Williams) 1890-1989
& John (Jack) Reginald Wallace 1892-1975

Jack Wallace was born in 1892, in Hamilton, Ontario, to William John Wallace (1863-1898) and Gertrude Alice Maude Kinnear (1866-1897). The family moved to Picton, Ontario, where Jack's sisters Greta Kinnear (1894), and Mary Gertrude Joyce (1896) were born.

Jack's parents died at a young age from tuberculosis so the children moved to Halifax to live with their paternal grandparents in 1897. Sadly, Joyce also died, aged three, in 1899, from diphtheria.

Violet Mary Williams was born in Quebec City in 1890. Her great-great-grandfather, Thomas Dunn, was the first Lieutenant-Governor of Lower Canada from 1805 to 1807. Her grandfathers were William Rhodes, a Member of the Quebec Legislature, and James William Williams, the fourth Bishop of Quebec. Her Father, Lennox Waldron Williams, was the sixth Bishop of Quebec and her mother was Caroline Anne (Nan) Rhodes.

L to R - Mary (Williams) Wallace with her father Lennox Williams, her sister Gertrude (Williams) Alexander and her cousin Dorothy (Rhodes) Evans, 1913

Mary grew up in Quebec City where activities would include family, church, and social gatherings, reading, card playing, knitting, and crocheting along with skating, tobogganing, tennis, and golf. She was an avid photographer and produced photo albums from Tadoussac where she spent her summers. For schooling, she attended King's Hall in Compton, Quebec.

Jack had a wonderful gift for mathematics. He went to work for the Bank of Montreal where he became a Chartered Accountant. He moved to Quebec City in his early twenties and, likely through a friendship with Jimmy Williams, he met Mary. Jack and Jimmy signed up together with the Canadian Expeditionary Force on September 20, 1915, in Levis and served with the 87th Battalion (Canadian Grenadier Guards) raised from Montreal and Quebec City.

Mary and Jack were engaged in 1916, prior to his heading off to World War I. Mary was an avid letter writer and they corresponded through the mail during his time overseas.

Following three months of training in England, Jack and Jimmy were deployed to France. Jimmy was killed on November 18th, 1916, on the last day of the Battle of the Somme. Jack would have been nearby when it happened. Later, on August 4th, 1917, Jack was wounded but was able to recover sufficiently to serve as staff of the 4th Canadian Division of the Canadian Army Corps for the rest of the war. He was promoted to Captain in 1918 and appointed aide-de-camp for the commander of the 4th Canadian Division, Major-General David Watson. He was discharged from the army on June 9th, 1919.

Within a week of Jack's return, Jack and Mary were married at the Cathedral of the Holy Trinity in Quebec. They immediately moved to Grand-Mère where Jack was employed as an accountant and assistant manager of the Laurentide Pulp and Paper Company, the town's only industry. Mary and Jack's three children were born during this time; Gertrude Anne (Nan) in 1920, John (Jackie) Williams in 1922, and Michael Sydney in 1927. Nan was born in the original Rhodes house at Tadoussac.

In Grand-Mère, the family were active members of St. Stephen's Anglican Church and avid golfers as members of the Laurentide

Mary (Williams) & Jack Wallace with their children: Nan, Jackie and Michael

Country Club. Mary proved to be a very proficient golfer, winning the Vice President's Cup in 1921. The famous golf course was originally built in 1910 with Van Horne money for Jack's company's employees, an excellent way to keep them healthy, happy, and fit.

Other activities of Jack's family included bridge playing, skiing, skating, and attending Saturday night dances. It was a good life, but there were economic downturns and mergers. The Laurentide Pulp and Paper Company was taken over by the Consolidated Paper Company and Jack moved the family to Montreal where he became an executive in the finance department. They moved to a very nice flat on Claremont Avenue in Westmount. Not long after, they moved to a Consolidated Paper Company house on Murray Hill Avenue. In 1938, they moved once again to an attractive, spacious, stone house on nearby Grenville Avenue, close to Murray Hill Park. Jack enjoyed sports and joined the Montreal Amateur Athletic Association, the Rackets Club of Montreal, and the Royal St. Lawrence Yacht Club. The family was active at St. Matthias Anglican Church in Westmount where Jack was a Warden.

At that time, Mary's father Bishop Lennox Williams, now a widower, came to live with their family until he died twenty years later in 1958.

Over the years, Nan, Jackie, and Michael had a special relationship with their grandfather. He had baptized each of them, was with them every summer at Tadoussac at the original Rhodes property where now *Brynhyfryd* is, and then lived with them in the same house in Westmount. The Wallaces grew up in a traditional Anglican environment.

Jack Wallace was a loving husband and father and a wonderful grandfather to his ten grandchildren. He cherished his many summers in Tadoussac with his family and Mary's very large extended family of cousins. He became known as Little Grandad to his grandchildren given that his father-in-law, Bishop Williams, Big Granddad, lived with them until 1958.

Jack had a wonderful sense of humour and played countless pranks to amuse the grandchildren. As an example, on a birthday occasion where a money birthday cake was served, Jack pulled a two-dollar bill out of his mouth, much to the astonishment of those at the table who would be lucky to find a nickel or dime in their cake serving.

Following the death of Mary's father in 1958 and after the children moved out, Mary and Jack moved to 646 Landsdowne Avenue in Westmount. Jack died there in 1975. He had lived a wonderful life despite it having been filled with much sadness, losing his parents and sister at a very young age, his best friend, and many friends during the war. Nevertheless, he had carried himself through life with grace. He was a very devoted Christian and a caring man in his community. He was loved by his family whom he cherished.

Mary was an avid card player and spent many hours playing with her grandchildren even into her late nineties. At dinners, she would sit with the older grandchildren at her end of the table for amusement and to be apprised of all the new trends and gossip. Afternoon teas were a favourite social time at the Wallace home.

Mary was active in the community on the Women's Guild at St. Matthias Church and headed up the Church and Tennis Club committees in Tadoussac. She was very astute at getting items actioned by bringing members onside with her proposals before raising them at a meeting.

She was an avid gardener, golfer, and bridge enthusiast. She was well-read and kept up to date on current events which she loved to discuss when people came to visit.

Mary was a gracious and God-loving person who was loved by all who knew her. In 1982 Mary moved to the Manoir Westmount. Following the death of her daughter, Nan, in 1983, she moved to Toronto where she could be close to her son Michael. Mary lived to the grand age of ninety-eight, as her father had.

Lance Corporal Herbert de Veaux Powel
1890-1915

Nothing is known of Herbert's earlier life when he must have come to Tadoussac along with his family. He was the son of Henry Baring Powel and brother to Harky Powel.

He became a soldier in the 2nd Company, 2nd Battalion, Eastern Ontario Regiment, 1st Brigade of the Canadian Expeditionary Force, and was a Lance-Corporal during the beginning of World War I. He went missing at the Battle of Langemarck during the second Battle of Ypres, on the western front. This was a battle in which the German army released its first gas attack. There was also heavy shelling and his body was never recovered. He is believed to have died on April 22, 1915.

Herbert Powel is commemorated in the First World War *Book of Remembrance* and there is a cross for him at the Menin Gate Memorial at Ypres.

Gertrude Isobel Morewood 1891-1977

Gertrude Isobel Morewood was born in Englewood, New Jersey, in 1891. She was the fourth child (of five) of Harry Morewood and Mary (Minnie) Rhodes, who was Col. Rhodes's sixth child and first daughter. Gertrude Isobel was known throughout her life as Bill or Billy. She trained as a nurse, but nothing is known about her working career.

When she was about eighteen years old, (1909) her parents moved the family to a house called *Benmore*, in Quebec City, which was the house her grandfather (Col. William Rhodes) had bought in 1848. It is believed that Billy was interested in a Jewish man for some time, but marriage to him was not acceptable to her mother, and Billy never married.

She loved small dogs and often had two. She was excellent at training them to do tricks and delighted many children by showing them what her dogs could do. She always kept a pack of small playing cards in her purse, and in her house, she kept a drawer full of toys to amuse visiting children. She was a keen gardener and there was a large garden at *Benmore* with vegetables in the middle of a huge square border of flowers. There was also a large lily pond at *Benmore* that had been created by Billy. The pond had not only lilies but also goldfish. In the fall she would capture as many goldfish as she could and they would spend the winter in a barrel in the basement at *Benmore*. In the spring she would usually find a few goldfish that had escaped the capturing procedure in the fall and had wintered in the pond, presumably by burrowing into the mud at the bottom.

When Harry and Frank Morewood were small children, their Aunt Bill took them to Tadoussac each summer to their Uncle Frank Morewood's newly built cottage, *Windward*. They would stay for a month under Billy's care thereby giving parents Bobby and Margaret a break. They travelled on the CSL boats to get there and back, which was probably a good thing as she was not a gifted driver. She was so short she actually looked *through* the steering wheel in her car so perhaps being able to see properly was a difficulty for her. Billy had a strong love for children and was adored by them in return. In Tadoussac she often took numbers of children out in the Williams's Whiteboat, rowing them about in the bay and around Pointe Rouge for picnics. Many people remember her joking and making kids laugh. She used to visit for days at a time when family members had babies, to help the mums in the first week or two at home. She was also known for helping older relatives as they became more helpless toward the end of their lives.

At the house on de Salaberry Avenue, Billy lived with her sister Nancy, who also never married. She was devoted to Nancy and looked after her until she died. The two of them used to make wooden jigsaw puzzles together. Aunt Bill, again, had a flower garden and a rock garden. After Nancy died in 1946, she invited her brother, Bobby, his wife, Margaret, and children Harry and Frank to live with her at that house. Frank was about twelve years old and Harry was fifteen at the time. Aunt Bill continued to be very much a second mother to the two boys.

There were a few disagreements between the two ladies of the house but it was mostly a harmonious relationship. The house had six bedrooms so there was plenty of room for everyone. Aunt Bill had a lifelong friend whom she had met when she was training to be a nurse, who became an Anglican nun. Sister Jane Frances, usually called Peg, was a frequent visitor at *Benmore* and the house on de Salaberry Avenue.

Billy's younger brother Bobby died in 1964. Aunt Bill and Margaret were alone – the boys now in their thirties had long since moved out – so they decided to sell the house and move into an apartment, not much more than a block away, on St. Louis Road.

Aunt Bill died in 1977, at the age of eighty-six.

Alexander Harcourt Carington Smith
1895-1975
& Mary Isabelle (Atkinson) 1911-1984

Lex, as he was known, was born in Quebec City in 1895 and was the eldest son of Robert Harcourt Smith and Mary Valliere (Gunn). He had two younger brothers, Gordon and Guy. He was educated at Bishop's College School in Lennoxville, Quebec.

In 1931 he married Mary Isabelle Atkinson in Levis, Quebec and they lived for many years on Pine Avenue in Quebec. He and Mary had one daughter, Susan, born in 1942. During World War II, Lex and Mary cared for two refugee children from England, Richard, and Elizabeth. They returned to their family in London after the war but the two families remained in touch for many years.

Mary was a talented knitter and a superb home chef as well as a community volunteer, especially with the Women's Auxiliary, and during the war, she even learned auto mechanics!

Lex was an importer and manufacturer's agent of fishing and

The Three Brothers, Guy, Gordon & Lex Smith

camping supplies and a long-time member of the Garrison Club in Quebec City. He was a keen outdoorsman and fisherman who tied his own flies. He was never happier than fishing at the Sainte Marguerite River with Uncle Art and his two brothers.

Lex and Mary purchased *Bayview Cottage* (now owned by the Stairs family) and it became known to the family as the fun place to be in Tadoussac. Mary was the most gracious hostess. Serving dinner to ten or fifteen family and friends was not unusual. They were great friends with Micheline Caron and George Kenilworth Craig who often stayed with Lex and Mary in the summer.

Lex died in 1975 in Quebec City. The last years of Mary's life were spent living with her daughter Susan and her husband Keith Robbins in and around Guelph, Ontario. Lex and Mary are buried in Mount Hermon Cemetery in Quebec City.

Sydney Waldron Williams 1899-1972

Sydney Williams was born in Quebec City in 1899 and was the fourth child of Bishop Lennox Waldron Williams and Caroline Annie Rhodes. Sydney had an older brother James (Jimmy) who died at the battle of the Somme in 1916 and older sisters Mary and Gertrude.

Sydney attended Quebec High School (Boy's School) from 1908 until 1916. He was Head Prefect and was awarded the Governor General's medal (for mathematics) and the Ann Ross Medal (for science). He attended Bishop's University from 1916 until 1918 and then the Royal Military College from 1918 until 1921 (College Number 1394). Sydney finished his degree in Chemical Engineering at McGill University (as RMC could not grant degrees at the time) graduating in 1923.

After graduation, Sydney worked for the Laurentide Paper Company in Grand-Mère between 1923 and 1927. He then decided to follow in the footsteps of so many of his ancestors by pursuing a degree in theology at Bishop's University (1927-1929). He was ordained a deacon in May 1929, and then a priest in 1930, by his father Bishop Lennox Williams at the cathedral in Quebec City.

After a short courtship, Sydney married Enid Price in June 1929. Enid's parents were Henry Edward Price and Helen Muriel (Gilmour). Enid's father, Henry, had been born in Talcahuano, Chile and, along with his brother William Price, had come to Canada as a child. Sydney and Enid had four children: Joan, Susan, Jimmy, and Sheila. Sydney was the curate for St Michael's Church in Bournemouth, England between 1930 and 1932 before returning to work as the curate at the Cathedral of the Holy Trinity in Quebec City while his father was Bishop. From 1933 until 1940 Sydney became the incumbent at St John the Evangelist, in Shawinigan Falls.

At the outbreak of war, and based on his previous military background, Sydney volunteered to serve and went overseas serving in the 66th Battery, 14th Field Regiment. While in England, Sydney worked as an instructor and he retired as a Major in 1944. He returned to his parish in Shawinigan as the Anglican Rector where he worked for many years until his retirement in 1967. In addition to an active

Enid & Sydney Williams at The Barn

Parish ministry, he served with great devotion on many Diocesan boards including the Executive Committee of Synod, Church Society, and the Pension Committee, as well as being a member of the Corporation of King's Hall, Compton.

Always a proud military man, in 1956, Sydney was made an Honorary Lt Col. of the 62nd Light Anti-Aircraft Regiment in Shawinigan. He was also the Honorary Chaplain for the RMC Club of Canada and would preside over many Remembrance Day Ceremonies at the College. The following quote comes from an article written for the RMC Review about Sydney: "His many friends knew him as a man of understanding and wit, and he is also remembered by a great many people for his help in times of their trouble. His strong faith and deep understanding enabled him to give both spiritual and practical comfort."

Sports were always a great interest of Sydney and as a young man, he was a member of the Bishop's University hockey and basketball teams. Sydney was also a great marksman and won many prizes for target shooting. He was a member of the Rifle Team at both RMC and McGill University and started the gun club in Shawinigan. Later in life, he taught the police in Shawinigan how to shoot. He used this skill in retirement when he could often be found shooting rats at the dump in Tadoussac.

Sydney spent his childhood summers in Tadoussac living with his parents. He was an avid golfer, tennis player, and canoeist. After his ordination, Sydney followed in the footsteps of his father by officiating the church services in July each summer until his retirement. Enid served as President of the Chapel Association for some years and contributed some of the needlepoint embroidery in the altar rail cushions.

On the death of his father, Sydney inherited *The Barn* and Sydney and Enid spent their retirement playing bridge with Coosie and Ray Price and enjoying their children and grandchildren. They had a strong friendship with Dr Taylor, an American clergyman who visited Tadoussac for many years.

Sydney died in St Anne's Military Hospital in 1972 and was buried in Mount Hermon Cemetery in Quebec City. The reredos (panel behind the altar) in the Protestant Chapel in Tadoussac, was presented in his memory by the congregation.

Sydney was a beloved minister, and his kind and friendly nature left a mark on everyone he met. Tadoussac was blessed to have had such a fine man as their liturgical leader for so many years.

Phyliss Frances Humphrys 1900-1974

Very little is known about Phyliss Frances Humphrys. Several people remember her name, but no details about her. It is thought that she first came to Tadoussac with the Languedocs. She stayed with Adele Languedoc at *Amberley*, and sometimes with Grace Scott at *Spruce Cliff*.

She was born in 1900 in Ottawa, Ontario. Her father, Beauchamp, was fifty and her mother, Clara, was thirty-eight when Phyliss was born. She had six brothers and two sisters. She died in 1974 in Ottawa and is buried in Beechwood Cemetery, the National Cemetery of Canada, with her parents and siblings. Her mother Clara was born in Quebec City in 1861, and her father in Montreal in 1849. Several of her siblings were born in Manitoba. Her father died when she was only one year old.

Coosie and Ray Price relaxing at their Maison Nicolas

Arthur Clifford (Coosie) Price 1900-1982
& Ethel Murray (Ray) (Scott) 1899-1987

"Count that day lost whose low descending sun
Views from thy hand no worthy action done."
-Margaret Olivia Slocum Sage

Coosie was the second of six surviving children of Amelia Blanche Smith and William Price. His siblings were: John Herbert (Jack), Charles Edward, Willa (Glassco), Richard Harcourt (Dick) and Jean (Trenier-Michel).

Ray was the second of four born to James Archibald Scott and Ethel Breakey. Her siblings were Harold, who was killed in World War I, John (Jack) and Mary (Warrington).

Coosie and Ray knew each other growing up - Coosie in Quebec City and Ray in Breakeyville. He attended Bishop's College School and school in England. In 1924 he graduated from the Royal Military

College of Canada and began his apprenticeship with Price Brothers. A fine athlete, he was on the RMC hockey team and won awards in other sports. In his final year, he was one of four Company Sergeant Majors.

Devoted to his father, he was with him the day he died in a landslide in Kenogami. By chance, he had, at that fateful moment, been sent to the mill to pick up mill plans. His father's death would change the course of his life as well as that of the entire Price family and the Price Brothers Pulp and Paper Company.

Thanks to many things, including a charmed life growing up in Breakeyville, Ray enjoyed more than her share of style and hosting skills. She also spoke French, a rarity amongst anglophones then living in Quebec.

In 1926 Coosie married Ray in the Presbyterian Church in Breakeyville. They could not be married in the Anglican Cathedral because Ray was a Presbyterian. Their first home was in Kenogami where their son Harold was born, then Quebec City where Tony, Scott and Willa (Lal) were born. In 1933 Coosie, now bankrupt, left Price Brothers and moved the family to Ottawa where he worked for the Eddy Company until he was asked, in 1939, to come back to Price Brothers as Vice President, Head of Sales. He became President in 1948, later Chairman and retired in 1964.

In 1949 Laval University honoured him with a Doctor of Laws Degree for leading the fundraising for University City. When his great friend Mathew Ralph Kane died leaving him much of his estate, he set up the Mathew Ralph Kane Foundation. Though the foundation is now part of the Citadel foundation, donations continue to focus on the Quebec and Saguenay/Lac St-Jean regions where Matt Kane and his family lived.

Coosie's mother died in 1947 leaving *Fletcher Cottage* to her two daughters. They sold it to their cousin Harky Powell. Harky later sold it to Bill Glassco (a son of Willa). *The Pilot House* was left to the four boys. They drew straws and Charlie won. After moving to Victoria B.C., Charlie sold the *Pilot House* to Coosie who by then had built *Maison Nicolas* (1948). A few years later Coosie transferred the *Pilot House* to his son Harold. All sales were 'token' – happy to keep the houses in the family.

Coosie and Ray shared a love of entertaining. They included all ages (Coosie, like his father, had a special affection for children) at the fishing cottages of Anse St Jean, Sagard and Lake Metis, excursions on *Jamboree III* and *IV*, cocktails on the deck of *Maison Nicolas*, and much more.

Coosie's day in Tadoussac often began with a round of golf with his cousin Harky Powel. When the Hotel stopped managing the Golf Course, Coosie put together arrangements to insure its continuation. He had great affection and admiration for the local families and could often be seen chatting with the regulars gathered on the bench in Pierre Cid's. Among his many pre- and post-retirement activities were salmon fishing (by all accounts, a renowned fly fisherman like his father), golf, boating, photography (award-winning), writing, oil painting and mushroom hunting.

Ray, a passionate gardener, coaxed flowers and vegetables out of small beds in the granite on which *Maison Nicolas* sits. Though she started life a stranger to the kitchen, she became a fine cook and was ahead of her time with her insistence on the freshest of everything – not easy in Tadoussac in those days. Her management of the galley on *Jamboree IV* was nothing short of heroic. She entertained visitors aboard who showed up in ports from Quebec City to Anticosti Island and Tadoussac to Chicoutimi and graciously accommodated a captain known for 'casting off' regardless of the weather forecast.

In their retirement years, they spent winters in Sonoma California with their daughter and family, spring and fall in Brockville and, as always, summers in Tadoussac. They shared a great love with family and friends throughout their fifty-six years together.

The Rev. Russell Dewart 1901-1997
& Ann (Stevenson) 1915-2008

Ann de Duplessis Stevenson was born in 1915 at 83 rue d'Auteuil in Quebec City, the daughter of Florence Louisa Maude Russell and Dr James Stevenson. The Stevenson sisters (Margaret, Ann, and Elizabeth) spent their childhood summers in Tadoussac staying at their grandmother's house in the village, the original family cottage *Spruce Cliff* built by their great-grandfather, Willis Russell in 1861. In 1922, Ann's father, Dr Stevenson, had their own cottage built for his family in Languedoc Park on land given to them by their cousin, Erie Russell Languedoc. This cottage now remains in Margaret's family and is owned by Margaret's son, Dennis Reilley. In the late 1920s, Dr Stevenson built a second cottage nearby which now remains in Elizabeth's family (the O'Neill house). In 1938, Ann married a Bostonian, Russell Dewart - coincidently her third cousin (Ann was a direct descendant of Willis Russell and Russell was a direct descendant of Willis's brother, William Russell). When one of Russell's sisters was getting married in Boston, Ann was sent to represent the Canadian branch of the family and was met at the train station by her future husband, Russell. Later, in the 1940s, Ann and Russell Dewart purchased *Tivoli*, the

Ann and Russell Dewart aboard a CSL Ship in 1945

Ann and Russell Dewart at Tivoli with the whole family 1950s

third Stevenson cottage (now the Dewart house). *Tivoli* has an interesting history. Shortly after World War I, Erie Languedoc had two square log cabins from the golf course moved on rollers to *Tivoli*'s present location where she joined them together and rented it out. It was then bought from Erie Languedoc by Professor Maclean from Rochester, NY, who named it *Tivoli*. In 1945, Ann and Russell purchased the cottage from the professor and continued summering there every summer with their six children, Timothy, Alan, Brian, Ted, Beth, and Judy. Many years later, in the mid-1980s, Russell and Ann built their own little chalet across the road from *Tivoli*.

Among Ann's additional pleasures were stimulating and philosophical conversations, exchanging aphorisms, delving into history, reading and writing, brisk walks, and sharing a cup of tea. Ann's time spent with family at her summer home in Tadoussac was a source of great joy and spiritual renewal. She authored a self-published memoir *Nose to the*

Window which included reflections, poems, letters, and anecdotes of her rich and vibrant life including much history of early Tadoussac and growing up in Quebec City.

Russell Dewart, was asked to tell of his life for his 50th college anniversary and part of what Russell wrote is below:

> "... after getting a delayed degree at Harvard, I took the rather conventional business route of selling everything from rubber boots to investment counselling. The salesman whom my long-suffering wife married turned up a few years later in the pulpit with a round collar, but with few of the other less discernible attributes usually associated with the Ministry. I regard this complete change of direction as one of the many paradoxes of my life and makeup.
>
> Having entered the Episcopal Seminary in Cambridge at the age of forty-three it was hard for me to believe that I had spent twenty-three years as a parish priest when I retired (for the first time). While a clergyman's life can be parochial and unexciting, I have found it a most challenging profession and one that is deeply rewarding.
>
> Perhaps the reason I say this is that the greatest joy I find in life is through my relationships with people of all ages and conditions - beginning of course with my own family and friends. The church records tell me that it has been my privilege to be called on to baptize, marry or bury some 1600 souls, and to present another 800 to the Bishop for Confirmation. These occasions for most individuals, as well as other times of tragedy and joy, are crucial and searching experiences. They are times when the clergyman is allowed to share some of the most significant moments in a family's life together. For him, they provide the unique opportunity to do what he was ordained to do – to walk along with his people as one who serves. Because of this, and for what he himself has learned from them – these times are never forgotten.
>
> My entire Ministry has been here in Massachusetts – at Epiphany, Walpole; Grace Church, Chicopee, and St. Peter's, Beverly. Since retiring in 1967, I have served part-time at the Old

North Church in Boston where my father was Rector fifty years ago, and more recently as Interim Pastor at St. John's, Beverly Farms. Throughout these years I have been blessed beyond measure with the kindness and appreciation of so many people in return for what little I on my own might give. God does work in mysterious ways.

Other activities during the past fifty years have centred largely around my family and home. Since the war, we have spent some part of most summers at our cottage in Tadoussac, Quebec – where the Saguenay River joins the St. Lawrence. It is here where my wife came as a child and where we as a family have spent some of our happiest days. Now our children return there with their children and friends – to the place they consider their first home.

We acquired our present home here, a small, cosy, New England house built originally by one Jeffrey Thistle, a planter, in 1668. Jeffrey built well but there is enough to keep me busy and happy in caring for his clapboard house and half-acre of land. It is here we expect to live out our days with occasional visits to our six children, and possibly further travel abroad if the spirit moves and the conditions are favourable.

But we are quite content to remain where we are. There is a good stack of Vermont hardwood outside for our fireplaces; there are some fish left in the ocean a half-mile away. And we are surrounded by friends. Fortunately, Ann and I still enjoy good health and, most of the time, our sense of humour. We are able to pursue our individual interests and to look forward not to vegetating, but to making the most of what time is left to us in being useful and helpful to others in our own particular way. The Lord has been good to us; our life together has been a full and happy one."

Russell Dewart served faithfully as a summer rector for twenty-one years (1953-1974). He died in 1997 and Ann died eleven years later in 2008. Both are buried in the family plot in Mount Hermon Cemetery, Quebec.

Noeline (Pixie) Winnifred (Smith) Palmer 1902-1986

Pixie Smith, daughter of George Carington Smith and Winnifred Dawes Smith, had one sister, Marion. She was born on Christmas Eve in 1902, and so was named Noeline. She strongly disliked her given name because she linked it to the children's nursery rhyme "Jack Spratt could eat no fat, his wife could eat no lean". Thus, due to her diminutive size, she came to be called Pixie.

Pixie grew up in Montreal, attended King's Hall, Compton, and then married Leonard Charles Dunlop Palmer (1898-1982). She and Leo moved to Ottawa in Rockcliffe Park and raised two children, George (1924-2019) and Linda born in 1930.

Leo's job with TWA involved taking care of visiting diplomats from around the world. Pixie was well-known in the Ottawa community as a gracious hostess and wonderful conversationalist. Her creative decorations for their annual Christmas party even made the Ottawa Citizen newspaper. Pixie was also a very accomplished seamstress.

Once George was grown, and following his career in theatre, Pixie often helped sew the costumes for The Ottawa Little Theatre Productions.

She and Leo travelled extensively throughout Europe. Pixie devoted her life to her family, supporting her husband in his career and then caring for Leo after he retired and when he suffered from PTSD due to his wartime experiences.

Pixie died in 1986, in Ottawa, and is buried in Beechwood Cemetery.

Doris & Jack Molson with their children, Verity & Robin

Doris Amelia Carington (Smith) 1902-1975 & Colin John Grasset Molson 1902-1997

C.J.G. "Jack" Molson was born in St. Thomas, Ontario to Mary Letitia Snider and Kenneth Molson. The family moved to Quebec City when Jack was two years old, where Kenneth worked as a manager for a branch of Molson's Bank. During Jack's childhood, he spent his summers with his grandparents (John Thomas Molson and Jenny Baker Butler) in Metis.

He learned to play the violin as a boy, and for his high school years, he attended boarding school at Ashbury College in Rockcliffe Park, near Ottawa. He went on to study economics and accounting, and as a young man, he was hired by Coopers & Lybrand.

Jack met Doris Amelia Carington Smith at a coming-out party aboard the HMS Hood, anchored in the Quebec harbour in August of 1924. (Built in 1922, it was the largest military vessel in the world at the time.) They fell in love and were married in Montmorency two years later.

Born in York (Toronto) on October 15, 1902, Doris was the first of three children whose parents were Charles Carington Smith (a Quebec City banker and first-generation Canadian in a family from Hertfordshire) and Aileen Dawson. Aileen's father, the renowned McGill scientist George Dudley Dawson, also had connections to Tadoussac in its earliest days as a summer resort.

Doris was raised in a sprawling Victorian house built at the top of Montmorency Falls. She had two younger brothers Noel and Herbert, and a younger sister May. As a girl, Doris took up figure skating, swimming, and golfing, and pursued these sports into her adulthood.

From the time of their wedding on, Jack would spend time with his family each summer in Tadoussac, where the Smiths had a summer home. Doris and Jack had two children: Robin, in 1929, and Verity in 1932. Jack owned a little wooden sailboat called *Lilith* but sold the vessel when the war started in 1939.

He became Paymaster for the Black Watch in Montreal. He and Doris continued to come to Tadoussac with their children through the war years' summers. After peace was declared in 1945, he bought land in Dwight Park and had a house built on it of his own design.

Doris was small and spirited, bright and energetic, and devoted to her family and her friends. She always had a much-adored dog whom she would train to do extraordinary tricks. Doris was especially known for her warmth and sociability, her concern for others, and her love for Tadoussac. Here, in the 1950s and '60s, she hosted bread-making parties where bread would be baked in their iconic outdoor clay oven, and her cocktail parties were always lively occasions.

Jack Molson continued to work as a chartered accountant in Montreal, while over the years his interest in Quebec's history and heritage grew. He became one of the founders of the Canadian Handicrafts Guild and was one of the first to support the efforts of Inuit carvers and printmakers. In 1955 when Westmount's *Hurtubise House* (built in 1714) was threatened with demolition, Jack mounted an effort to save the island's oldest home. He persuaded his friend, James Beattie, and his aunt, Mabel Molson, to help him buy the house. In the next few years, he purchased two other properties, including natural sites in Gaspé that were vulnerable to commercial development. By 1960 the Canadian Heritage of Quebec was incorporated and had an active board of professionals as directors. The CHQ foundation, under Jack's direction, would save the *Simon Fraser House* in Ste. Anne-de-Bellevue, the *Laterriere Seigneurial Mill* at Les Eboulements in the Charlevoix, as well as *Les Rochers*, Sir John A. Macdonald's summer home in St. Patrick, and dozens of other heritage properties on both sides of the St. Lawrence River, including Bon Désir and Point à Boisvert on the north shore.

Here in Tadoussac, Jack Molson and James Beattie purchased the *Pilot House* (a brick Molson-Beattie House located near Anse a l'Eau) with the intention of converting it into a museum. When historical fishing vessels and sailboats were donated to the CHQ foundation, Jack had barns erected on land behind the *Pilot House* in order to preserve them. He bought land above the sand dunes which he later donated to the Saguenay-St. Lawrence Marine Park and also the Hovington farm which is still active today overseen by the local Municipal Regional Council. He was also very supportive of the Tadoussac Protestant Chapel.

In 1979 Jack Molson was awarded the Order of Canada for his dedication to historical preservation through the Canadian Heritage of Quebec. By then, he had long retired from his work in order to devote all of his time to the foundation. In spite of his remarkable vision of the future and all of his accomplishments, Jack was a modest man who shied away from personal publicity. His manner was unassuming, his personal life pared down to the essentials. One of the things he loved the most was a simple picnic on a St. Lawrence River beach with some boiled eggs and a cup of tea brewed in a billycan over a small fire. On more than one occasion he was known to have said to Doris, "This is a beautiful, unspoiled spot. It would be such a pity if someone decided to develop it. We should buy it."

Doris adored Tadoussac. Early every morning, weather permitting, she would go down the path in front of their cottage to the beach for a bracing swim in the bay. Later she would rouse up friends and neighbours

Jack Molson with daughter Verity circa 1934

for picnics, or Sunday evening bonfires on Indian Rock. She was also a mainstay of the Tadoussac Protestant Chapel, where, when she wasn't playing the organ herself, she sat as close to the organist as possible so that her singing voice would give encouragement to the player.

Her faith was strong. Had Doris been able to choose the manner of her passing, she may well have chosen to go the way she did. On July 14, 1975, she was enjoying a game of golf at the Tadoussac Golf Club with her best friends when she began to feel dizzy. She sat down; her heart failed; her friends gathered around her. She was seventy-two.

Predeceased by Doris, and his daughter Verity in 1995, Jack Molson passed away peacefully after a long illness in 1997. He was ninety-five.

Helen Florence Price 1902-1981

Helen was born in Quebec in 1902, the eldest daughter of Henry Edward Price and Helen Gilmour. She spent her many summers in Tadoussac, growing up with ten younger siblings and at many times looking out for them. Helen had an active and outgoing life and kept up on all news of the family. She lived in Toronto where facing the hardships of the Great Depression, she worked and for some years served as the Matron for the Junior school at Upper Canada College.

In her later years in Tadoussac, she often stayed with her good friend Grace Scott. She had many nieces and nephews, some of whom knew her well, remembering her appearing in pantaloons and black stockings. For one of her nieces, she was there to drive her to the hospital to have her baby. For another, Aunt Helen made the arrangements for her niece and her husband to spend their honeymoon in Tadoussac during the month of April. She was always interested in others, very generous and wanted to help whenever possible.

Aunt Helen would never be forgotten by those who knew her.

Florence Blanche Willa (Price) Glassco
1902-1991

Florence Blanche Willa Price, a much longed-for daughter, was born on a hot 24th of August in 1902 in her parent's home at 575 Grand Allée in Quebec City. Her birth would have been celebrated by her older brothers Jack, Coosie, and Charlie, and her parents, Sir William and Lady Amelia Blanche (Smith).

A fair-skinned redhead, Willa was as comfortable wrestling with her brothers and climbing trees as she was learning the arts of the fairer sex. She loved to dance and sing by her father's side at the piano and there was much music in the ever-expanding family. By the time she was four, the family was completed by Dick and her sister Jean. At only six, a bout of scarlet fever left Willa quite deaf and turned this rambunctious child timid.

Summers were spent in Tadoussac where her mother had insisted Sir William turn what had been a bawdy boarding house for his Price Brothers' managers into a family retreat. After extensive renovations, *Fletcher Cottage* became the clubhouse for the six Price children and their raft of cousins and friends. Governesses would be charged with organising picnics and hikes and swimming, boating, and fishing trips. Meals would be simply prepared and served to the children on the porch on the northeast side of the house with the children sleeping in bunks in the open porch above. There are names still in evidence, carved into the cedar shingles on the outside of the porch. Lady Price and her friends would play bridge, tennis, and golf, go to church, and have costume parties and cocktail parties. The summers were long-from May to the end of September - and they would travel up on the CSL steamship from Quebec with trunks and staff.

Willa's education in Quebec would have been in English, Victorian in tone, and with little expectation of her going to college or university. She, along with many of her peers at eighteen, was sent to England to be presented at court to King George V and Queen Mary and then enjoyed a leisurely tour of Europe and all its sites.

At age twenty-two, tragedy struck the family. Sir William, her much-loved father, was killed in a landslide in Kenogami. It changed everything for her siblings and mother and Willa dedicated herself to the care of her mother. At twenty-five, Willa met and married Grant Glassco, a promising young businessman from Winnipeg who had just begun his career as a chartered accountant, and they settled in Forest Hill in Toronto. They went on to have four children, June, Gay, Dick, and Bill with Willa insisting she return to Quebec for each pregnancy to have her care and delivery at her mother's house. And then, like her mother before her, she brought her family every summer to Tadoussac for tennis, golf, church, picnics, and swimming.

After the Second World War, Grant and Willa purchased a working farm near Kleinberg, just north of Toronto, and the family spent weekends there, where driving a tractor was as important a skill as any in this family. Willa was involved in her communities and church, forming long attachments with her neighbours. She was a woman who had fierce, loyal friendships that lasted her long life. These she had at the farm, in town, and in Tadoussac. Up until her last year, when in Tadoussac she would always make a point to go and have tea with her brother Coosie, her cousins, and her many childhood friends still living in the village. Her French was perfectly tuned to the familiar Tadoussac dialect.

Grant and Willa had help at home, bringing Eva Drain into the family in the 1950s. Eva, an orphan, had come to Canada from London's East End as a Bernardo's baby, starting her employment at age eight with her brother at a Montreal match factory. After serving as a maid with the Reverend Scott, she started with Willa and Grant and stayed with Willa all her life. Eva was devoted to the whole family and as grandchildren, we have many memories of Eva, the devout storyteller and dog lover who was so much a part of our family.

Willa beamed. Her smile was infectious, and she often threw her head back laughing. She could control her brood and twenty grandchildren with a firm hand, but she was more at home being the optimist with an insatiable sense of adventure. She was an avid traveller, she and Grant travelling and living in Brazil in their 40s and 50s where he had business interests. She loved the theatre and when her youngest son, Billy, a theatre director, started the Tarragon Theatre in Toronto,

Willa proudly attended every performance, no matter how scandalous the plays might be.

Grant contracted lung cancer and died at only sixty-three, leaving Willa a widow for the next twenty-three years. She experienced a sort of renaissance. Released from her domestic duties she travelled to England to visit her sister, Jean and her family. She spent months in Tadoussac and up at the farm. She dated a number of very charming gentlemen and spent time with friends. She would hold a yearly picnic at the farm for the Canadian Hearing Society, a charity she was active in all her life. The family would be wrangled into putting on a massive spread as families of the hard of hearing would converge for an annual outdoor gathering that was the highlight of the season.

Willa was always up for an adventure, for a dance, she wrote in her journal every day and recounts a life that was truly well spent.

She tragically died driving back from the farm just days after her 89th birthday. She went through a stop sign. She surely had another good decade in her at least and it was a blow to everyone when she left.

She was warm, loving, and attentive. Intelligent and curious. She had a very strong sense of right or wrong and believed in the best in people. Though tiny in stature and frame she could hug the breath out of a grown grandson. She is missed.

Grace Scott at Spruce Cliff

Francis Grace Scott 1904-1993

Francis Grace Scott was born in 1904, in Quebec City. She lived there until the age of eight when her family moved to Kenmore, New York. She was the daughter of Mabel Emily Russell and Charles Cunningham Scott.

Grace taught English at Kenmore West High School for almost forty years. Kenmore was a suburb of Buffalo. Never having married, she lived in the same house for her whole life, looking after her parents.

Grace had a commanding presence and was strict and disciplined. Her niece, Susie, recalls summers in Tadoussac were quite structured and very social. Grace loved to know what was going on in the village and the door was always open for people to come and visit. For many years she was the President of the Tadoussac Protestant Chapel. One of her lasting legacies is taking Susie to church every Saturday morning to play the organ and practice the hymns for church on Sunday.

Grace also had high ideals and morals reflecting the times she grew up in. She was an avid reader and always liked to discuss what people had just read, current events and American politics!

She was a devoted lover of dogs and had several black cocker spaniels. She loved to sit on the back porch with a dog on her lap, looking at the view.

Grace loved Tadoussac and couldn't wait to get there every summer. She inherited *Spruce Cliff* from her mother Mabel Emily Russell Scott. When summering in Tadoussac, Helen Price, Lily Bell Rhodes, and Adele Languedoc would often stay with her at *Spruce Cliff*. Her niece, Susie (Scott) Bruemmer also spent many summers staying with her and eventually inherited the cottage.

Grace died at the age of eighty-eight in 1993 in Kenmore, N.Y. And is buried in Mount Hermon Cemetery in Quebec City with her parents.

Monica Rhodes 1904-1985

Monica Rhodes was born in 1904, in Sillery, Quebec. Her father was Armitage Rhodes (born in 1848) and her mother was Katie von Iffland of Sillery, Quebec, the daughter of Reverend von Iffland and the second wife of Armitage Rhodes. She was the sister of Armitage (Peter) Rhodes and half-sister of Dorothy Rhodes and Charlie Rhodes.

Monica's father, Armitage, died in 1909 and a couple of years later her mother took her young family to England. She lived first in Caterham, Surrey, where she attended Eothen School, along with Imogen Holst, daughter of the musician and composer Gustav Holst. After the end of the First World War, her family moved to St Marychurch, Devon, and finally, after her younger sister's marriage, to Chiddingfold, Surrey.

After her mother died in 1938, Monica studied at St Christopher's College, Blackheath to be able to work for the Anglican Church in Canada. She served as a Bishop's Messenger in Manitoba. She was deeply religious and after she retired, she moved to the Town of Mount Royal where she was a member of St. Peter's Anglican Church.

Monica often stayed with her sister Dorothy, Grace Scott, and at Boulianne's Hotel during the summer in Tadoussac.

Monica is interred in the Rhodes family plot at Mount Hermon Cemetery in Sillery, Quebec.

George Noel Carington Smith 1904-1988

The second of four children and eldest son of Charles and Aileen Carington Smith, Noel was born on Christmas Day and aptly named. The family lived at Montmorency Falls, where Noel's lifelong love of the countryside was nurtured. There are stories of fifteen or twenty feet of snow in the winter - he had his own dog and sledge to cope with this - of eating maple syrup turned to a crispy mouthful in a bowl of deeply frozen snow, and of the magic of living close to the amazing waterfall which famously produces a huge cone of frozen spray in the winter. He was educated at Lower Canada College and then Upper Canada College, graduating in 1922. The next three years were spent training at the Royal Military College at Kingston.

Noel decided to make his career in the British Army and in 1925 he moved to the United Kingdom and joined the Royal Artillery Regiment. As a young army officer, he was stationed in various places within the UK. In 1929 he was stationed in India and spent an interesting and active two years there. While there he famously shot dead a 'man-eating' tiger that had killed two people in the local village. In those days this was a wonderful thing to have done, and he became quite a local hero.

Even though the Royal Artillery was highly mechanized during the 1930s, horse riding ability was apparently considered very desirable, and Noel proved to be fully capable of reaching an excellent standard. He took part in many horse races, often won, and had many silver trophies to display. When he was still new to British Horse Racing, his future father-in-law bet on him. At the end of the successful race, it turned out that this was the only winning ticket, so the odds were excellent. A win that boded well for his future, no doubt.

It was in 1934 that he met Mary Falconer Donaldson, the youngest daughter of a Scottish shipowner, and in 1936 they were married. Army life involved a lot of moving around, and Noel and Mary were no exception. They had four children, Charles Falconer born in 1938, and Katherine Ann in 1940, at which point Mary and the two young children sailed the Atlantic to live in Kingston, Ontario, where they stayed until 1944. After the war, and by now back in Scotland, twins

Robert and Rosemary were born in 1945.

At the start of the war, Noel was the adjutant attached to a reserve Technical Assistance (T.A.) unit based in County Durham in the north of England, however, within a few months, he was posted to Kingston, as a Staff College instructor. After this, he commanded an artillery regiment during the invasion and conquest of Sicily. Later experiences included Anzio and Ortona. Just at the end of the war, he spent a short time in England, before his second spell in India. Here he became the Acting Commandant of the British Army College in Quetta, in what is now Pakistan, during the months leading up to Independence and Partition; a job that involved overseeing the movement of many thousands of Hindus to the south into safety in India - a huge logistical job, involving the requisitioning of several trains.

In 1947 Noel decided to leave the army and he took up a civilian post in Perth, Scotland, administering the T.A. branch of the Scottish regiment, The Black Watch. He still loved riding, and for a while became Master of the Perthshire Drag Hunt. After six years he and Mary bought an arable farm, on which they built a new family-sized farmhouse, and Noel became a full-time farmer. There followed many happy years of farming, breeding Aberdeen Angus beef cattle and Scottish black-face sheep. Noel taught his children to ride, fish, and shoot, passing on his love of sports, horses, dogs, and the outdoors. He could now enjoy fishing and shooting too, and taking part in these two sports was something he continued after he retired from farming until his death in 1988.

Adele de Guerry Languedoc 1904-1993

On Sunday, August 5th, 2007, the congregation of the Tadoussac Protestant Chapel laid a headstone in memory of Adele de Guerry Languedoc on the chapel grounds. Adele was born in Tadoussac in the early 1900s and summered here with her family throughout her life. Adele's stepmother, Erie Russell Janes Languedoc, was the granddaughter of Willis Russell who, along with Colonel Rhodes, were among the first to build summer cottages at Tadoussac in the 1860s. Erie purchased the lands that later became known as Languedoc Park after she married the widower, George de Guerry Languedoc. The four original cottages in Languedoc Park were Erie's cottage and the cottages of the three Stevenson sisters who were great-granddaughters of Willis Russell.

At the time of her death, she was remembered by the National Archives of Canada for her distinguished career as a librarian. Her career began with her undergraduate degree at McGill University including a library diploma and she received a Bachelor of Library Service from Columbia University in 1946.

Adele served for five years with the American Relief for France during the Second World War and her efforts helped to restore the regional libraries that had been so damaged during the war. She also set up the first children's library that existed outside Paris.

On her return to Canada, she was hired as an 'Accessions Librarian' at the Canadian Bibliographic Centre which was later named the Library and Archives of Canada. She

Adele at a picnic

helped to build our now-famous collection of Canadian literature and documents. She was named Assistant National Librarian in 1964. Through her work in Ottawa, she was asked to represent Canada as a member of the UNESCO seminar on libraries and served as a consultant in Africa. The National Library News wrote of her at the time of her death "To all her work, she brought a broad, deep knowledge and experience of Canada's French and English tradition."

Adele is remembered by her friends in Tadoussac as a friendly, smiling member of the community sitting on her porch at her cottage in Languedoc Park. Few realized what important work she had done at the National and International levels. She was a neighbour and a friend.

Herbert Carington Smith 1906-1966

Known as Herbie, Herbert Carington Smith was the third of four children born to Charles and Aileen Carington Smith. The family lived at Montmorency Falls, where he told of a life of skiing and skating to school, canoeing on the river, and sailing in the sea. Like his brother Noel, Herbie was an accomplished horse rider, and when he lived in Hereford, England, much later in life, he used to run the local pony club and annual camp.

His engineering skills started early when he and a friend built a wall across a road one night, and on another occasion, craned a car onto the top of a roof when they tired of the boastful chap who owned it!

He went to the Lower and Upper Canada College, before spending four years training at the Royal Military College in Kingston.

Following in brother Noel's footsteps, Herbie joined the British Army as a Royal Engineer and studied at Cambridge University. From 1930 he was posted to Ordnance Survey Companies at Fort Southwick, Southampton, and Edinburgh. In 1931 he took part in a Trans-Atlantic Ocean race with the Royal Engineers. He had the last crew position as a cook and had to hastily ask his mother for cookery lessons! He told of having to put the dough for the bread in a tin, and take it to bed with him to make it rise.

In 1933 he took part as a surveyor in an Oxford and Cambridge University expedition to Spitzbergen.

In 1935 Herbie spent two and half years with the British Guiana-Brazil Boundary Commission. Then he served as Captain for another eighteen months with the 19th Field Survey Company, which included a tour in France with the British Expeditionary Force. He worked at survey and training centres in Scarborough, Derby, and then Ripon, as an instructor in Fields Works and Bridging. He also obtained his pilot's licence at that time.

Following this, he again visited Spitzbergen for special duties with Force 111, a joint Canadian, British and Norwegian operation largely composed of Canadian Sappers sent to evacuate the inhabitants, destroy fuel stocks and render all facilities useless to the enemy. He received a mention in despatches for saving a Sunderland flying boat from being driven ashore in a storm. He collected some French-Canadian soldiers, none of whom had ever handled an oar before and took out a small rowing boat. With that, he was able to get a line to the Sunderland and tow it to safety.

He then went as General Staff Officer (Grade 1) on a liaison mission to Australia, where he was highly regarded, working with Australian and US intelligence. He served as a Special Operations Executive, and Officer of Strategic Services, taking part in the top-secret behind-the-lines network. His experience included battles at Salamanca, during August and September of 1943, Finischafen and Lae in September of 1943, The Admiralty Islands in March 1944, and Hollandia in April of 1944. He got experience being in charge of staff and working with Aerial Photography, Combined Ops, Jungle Warfare, Airborne, Mortars and Pioneer duties.

He was in charge of small pockets of men, walking in and out of the jungle multiple times during 1943 and 1944 on missions that are still highly classified. It would seem that he was in Force 136, a far eastern branch of the British World War II intelligence organisation. Royal Engineers were involved in building the bridge over the River Kwai in 1942 and 1943.

His next foreign tour took him back to the Far East as CRE to the British and Indian Divisional Engineers, British Commonwealth Occupation Force in Japan, and then in May 1948, to Command of the Engineer Training Centre, FAREFLY at Kluan, Malaya, until November of 1952.

In Japan in 1947, the Lt Gen. Commander in Chief of the British Commonwealth Occupation Force recommended him for the Order of the British Empire for his meritorious service in carrying out his duties most efficiently, making troops comfortable, hard-working, taking a keen interest in his work and because his mechanical aptitude was excellent.

"Success of the engineering work in this formation 268 Indian Infantry Brigade Group, is entirely due to the organizational capacity of Colonel Smith and his untiring zeal and energy to see the task through. He carried out his task despite the great difficulties of lack of any precedence and procedure. He had to organize the procurement of the Engineer Store which in itself was a complicated task and needed an officer of Colonel Smith's calibre."

In 1948, he was awarded Officer of the Most Excellent Order of the British Empire following his engineering work and organizational skills in the Far East. He was mentioned in despatches in December 1949. His medals included The Pacific Star, British War Medal ribbons, France & Germany Star, and the Italy Star.

Herbie met Alison (Ty) Gatey, a Major in the First Aid Nursing Yeomanry, also working in intelligence, and they married in London in 1950. Their son, Anthony, was born in Malaya in 1951. Herbie used to love getting parcels from his sisters in Canada – they used to send blocks of maple sugar - and he loved slicing this on his porridge. He passed his love of swimming, rowing, riding and dogs on to his son and daughter.

Herbie returned to the UK in May 1953 on promotion to Colonel, as Assistant Director of the Directorate of Royal Engineers at the Ministry of Supply in London. He had a passionate love of sailing and the sea, and as a member of the Royal Engineers Yacht Club, he was Skipper of the *Right Royal*. In the 1956 Channel Race, he saved the yacht, which was dismasted in a gale. He refused to abandon ship, despite offers to be taken off, and got the boat and crew, battered but safe, into Dunkirk. His final posting, in 1957, was as Commanding Officer of the Special Air Service base in Hereford, although it was officially known as the Territorial Army base. Herbie retired in 1960.

When he retired from the Army Herbie spent some time working as a surveyor on the M4 motorway that was being built. He and Ty then moved to Keswick. He enjoyed rowing on the lake and climbing the mountains. The family used to go on a narrowboat every year on the canal. When his daughter was seven, he saved her life when she fell overboard and became trapped between the boat and the canal bank. He hooked her out with the boat hook.

He was a warden at Crosthwaite Church in Keswick. He loved

seeing his brother Noel and family in Scotland, and his sister Doris came over to England in 1954. He had plans to take the family to Canada in 1966, but sadly became ill that year and passed away just before his 60th birthday.

His varied career well reflected his ever-inquiring mind, objectivity and problem-solving. A man of immense courage, with unfailing good humour and quiet enthusiasm, earned him universal respect and made him many friends.

Gordon Carington Smith 1906-1974

Family, dedication to the Canadian Armed Forces, and Tadoussac were the most important things in the life of Gordon Carington Smith.

Gordon was born in 1906 in Quebec City to Robert Harcourt Smith and Mary Valliere (Gunn) Smith. He was the second of three sons. His older brother was Alexander (Lex) and his younger brother was Guy.

They enjoyed a happy childhood growing up on Grande Allée in the English area of Quebec City. In 1911 the family purchased *Dufferin House* and so began the family love affair with Tadoussac.

Following the family tradition, Gordon was educated at Bishop's College School in Lennoxville, and the Royal Military College in Kingston, from which he graduated in 1927. He completed his

Gordon Smith (in window) aboard Penwa

engineering degree at McGill in 1929.

Immediately, Gordon joined the Royal Canadian Artillery and was appointed a Lieutenant with the Royal Canadian Horse Artillery with which he remained until the beginning of World War II. He then joined the staff of General Worthington and participated in the formation of the Royal Canadian Armoured Corps at Camp Borden.

On April 30, 1941, while on his way to England to begin his war service, Gordon's ship the S.S. Nerissa was torpedoed off the coast of Ireland in the middle of the night. After spending some time in the water helping lift others into a lifeboat he was rescued and proceeded to London. Gordon then served in the Italian Campaign and was twice wounded in action, once while second in command of the British Columbia Dragoons. He served in the liberation of France and ended the war at the Canadian General Reinforcement Unit in Britain.

He returned to Canada and his first posting was in Halifax, followed by Kingston, Washington DC, and his final posting was in Ottawa. He received an Honorary Discharge in March 1959.

Following his retirement, Gordon and his family moved to Halifax where he joined the architectural firm of Dumaresq and Byrne. He was a loyal board member of the Canadian Corps of Commissionaires, the Royal Commonwealth Society, and the United Institute of Canada.

In 1933 Gordon married Jacqueline Dumaresq of Halifax. They had two children, a son Arthur Harcourt Carington Smith in 1934, and a daughter Eve D'Auvergne Smith in 1939. There were also five grandchildren, Gordon and Christopher Smith and Donald, Janet and Ted McInnes.

After family and career, Gordon's main love was Tadoussac. Whenever possible he and his family would make the trip to Tad. He had sold his share of *Dufferin House* to Guy Smith in the 1930s so he and his family enjoyed many different cottages. His pride and joy, was his Cape Island boat, *Penwa*. He was never happier than being in Tad and spending time with his extended family, especially his two beloved brothers. That was his heaven!

Gordon died in Halifax in 1974, aged sixty-eight, and is buried there in Fairview Cemetery.

Marion Sarah (Smith) Dobson 1907-1992

Marion, or Mally as she was called in Canada, was born in 1907 in Montreal. Her parents were George Carington Smith and Winifred Dawes Smith, and she had one sister, Pixie. She grew up on Dorchester Avenue in Montreal and attended King's Hall, Compton. Her summers were spent in Tadoussac with her many Smith and Price cousins.

In 1929, in Montreal, she married Benjamin Arthur Palin Dobson and moved to Heaton Lodge, Bolton, Lancashire in England. She would live the rest of her life in England but made frequent visits to Canada and particularly Tadoussac.

She and Ben had three sons. Bob was born in 1931, Chris in 1936, and Andrew in 1942. She had five grandchildren, Richard, Caroline, Jonathan, Nick, and Alexandra (Alex). After Ben's death in 1962, Marion continued to live in their family home, *Whitestock*, in the Lake District. Their son Bob took over the family home in the late 1970s or early 1980s and Marion moved to a cottage in the Cotswolds to be near Chris and his wife Pen. In 1982, she moved into a cottage on Chris and Pen's property and was there until her death in 1992.

Marion was smart and interested in everything, especially anything political. She was very politically astute. She rose up the ranks of the Conservative Party and eventually became Chair of the Northwest area of England. This was a huge volunteer job for which she was awarded the Order of the British Empire (OBE) in 1960 for "Political Services." Her interest in, and knowledge of, politics never waned. She was also a volunteer for the Bolton Nursing Association, the Royal College of Nursing, and the Bolton Hostel Committee.

To quote her daughter-in-law, Pen, "She was a wonderful, loving, caring woman."

Robert Guy Carington Smith 1908-2006
Constance Isobel (Price) Smith 1908-1944
Jean Alexandra (McCaig) Smith 1903-1988

Known to most in Tadoussac as either Poppa or Uncle Guy, Robert Guy Carington Smith was born in 1908, in Quebec City, to Robert Harcourt Smith and Mary Valliere (Gunn) Smith. He was the third of three sons. His older brothers were Alexander (Lex) and Gordon. They enjoyed a happy childhood growing up on Grande Allée in the English area of Quebec City. In 1911 Robert Harcourt Smith purchased *Dufferin House* in Tadoussac, Quebec as a summer home, from Henry Dale of Poughkeepsie, N.Y. After being ceded to all three boys, Guy bought out his brothers' stake in the house, and *Dufferin* remained in the family for four consecutive generations.

Like his brothers before him, Guy was educated at Bishop's College School in Lennoxville, Quebec, and the Royal Military College in Kingston, Ontario, from which he graduated in 1929. Guy also attended McGill University for Economics from 1929 to 1930. After his time at McGill University, Guy entered the Department of Trade and Commerce as a Junior Trade Commissioner in 1930.

"Iso" was born in 1908, in Quebec City to Henry Edward Price and Helen Muriel Gilmour. Her siblings included Helen Florence (1902), Enid Muriel (1904), Millicent Ruth (1906), William Gilmour (1910), James Cuthbert (1912), Sheila Hope (1914), Henry Edward (Ted) Clifford (1916), Llewellyn Evan (1919), and Barbara Joan (1921), all born in Quebec City.

During her young life, Iso saw the passing of her younger sister Barbara Joan at the age of three in 1924, her brother Gilmour in 1940 at the age of thirty, and Evan in 1944 at the age of twenty-five. Despite this, or perhaps because of it, the family grew up close in the English section of Quebec City.

At the age of twenty-three Isobel travelled alone to Buenos Aires, Argentina, where on April 27, 1932, she married Guy Smith who was stationed in the Canadian Diplomatic Service. They had three children during their marriage: Valliere Ann (1933) and Susan Pamela (1935) in

Guy Smith sailing Hobo

Buenos Aires, and Penelope Joan (1939) in Rye, New York.

In 1931 Guy was posted to Buenos Aires as the Assistant Trade Commissioner and then to New York in 1936. Guy was granted a leave of absence from 1940 to 1945 to join the Royal Canadian Artillery in the war effort. During his time of service, Guy was involved in a motorcycle accident that took him out of active service. At the time of his discharge, Guy had earned the rank of Lieutenant-Colonel.

Sadly, Iso passed away at the age of thirty-six in 1944, in Ottawa, Ontario. Constance Isobel Smith is buried at the Mount Hermon Cemetery in Quebec City.

Jean, Mumsie, Aunt Jean, Grannie was born in Quebec in 1903. Her parents were John and Evelyn McCaig. She had two sisters, Ruth, born in 1908, and Ester, and one brother, William John, born in 1911.

The family moved to Edmonton, Alberta in 1911. Jean trained as a stenographer and early in her adult life, she developed a love of travel. During the 1920s and 1930s, she visited Vancouver, Honolulu, San Francisco, Berkeley, South Hampton, and Brazil and settled finally in New York in the early 1940s.

She was working as a stenographer in the Canadian Consul General/ Trade Commissioner's office when she met Robert Guy Carington Smith. They were married on December 12, 1945.

In 1946, Guy was appointed to Havana, Cuba, to continue his diplomatic and trade service. From there, Guy enjoyed a robust career as a Canadian diplomat travelling to posts in many different countries including Rome, London, Paris, Washington, Tokyo, the West Indies, and finally, back to New York where he was appointed as Consul General for Canada for the states of New York, New Jersey, and Connecticut. For the next twenty years, Jean travelled to, and lived in all these places and became a gracious hostess for Guy as he pursued his diplomatic career.

Following his retirement, Guy and Jean moved to Brockville, Ontario where he remained highly involved in both civic and church duties. Always a dedicated subject of the Queen, Poppa faithfully corresponded using only Queen's head stamps.

After career and family, Poppa's main love was *Dufferin House* in Tadoussac. Not a summer went by without Poppa spending it in Tadoussac tending the gardens and managing the property. For a while, a main fixture of the house was the old English taxi ("Gertrude") that Poppa would drive around the streets of Tadoussac heading to church or a run to the local store. It was Tadoussac's version of Jessica Tandy and Morgan Freeman from Driving Miss Daisy with Jean in the back waving to us all!

Jean died in Brockville in 1988 and Guy in 2006, aged ninety-eight, and is buried at the Mount Hermon Cemetery in Quebec City near Jean and Isobel.

Smut the Dog, Emily (Bethune) Evans, Kae Evans, Elizabeth, Maggie and Ann (Stevenson), May Carrington Smith and Nan Gale at Cap à Jack

Katherine Evans 1909-2001

Kae Evans was the only child of Basil Evans, (the second son of Dean Lewis Evans) and Muriel Curtis. She lived in Montreal with her parents on Bruce Avenue. In Tadoussac, as a youth, she stayed with her grandfather at the Beattie house and later in life she was a frequent visitor in her uncle Trevor's house, *Ivanhoe*, opposite the golf course clubhouse.

While she never married or had children of her own, she took a great interest in her many cousins and nieces and nephews. Her Christmas presents were famous for being homemade and often unusual. Any parcel marked "with love from Muriel and Kae" was bound to be a surprise and always opened with great anticipation.

Kae spent much of her life caring for others, particularly her parents. She nursed her father until he died in the early 1960s and then her mother a decade after that. For years she lived alone in an apartment on Ste Catherine Street West, in Montreal.

There used to be two very old flags hanging in the chancel of the chapel that are historic but were in very poor condition. When Kae died she left a generous sum of money to the chapel and it was used for the professional restoration and display of the two flags. They can now be seen at the back of the church in glass cases.

Kae's ashes are interred in the Evans family plot in the Mount Royal Cemetery with her grandfather.

William Gilmour (Gilly) Price 1910-1940

William Gilmour (Gilly) Price was the fifth child and the eldest son out of ten children of Henry Edward Price and Helen Muriel Gilmour. Muriel was the granddaughter of John Gilmour who was a contemporary of the original William Price and an equally renowned lumber merchant in Quebec City at that time.

The Harry Prices lived at 2 and then 16 St. Denis Ave, near the Citadelle. At the time they were comfortably off during Gilly's childhood, as his sister Helen talked of trips to Europe in 1913, 1921 and 1928. Gilmour attended Trinity College School, Port Hope from 1924 to 1928. After leaving TCS, he lived with his parents, and according to his family, he loved children and had a wonderful rapport with them. Later, during the depression, the family lost their money with the bankruptcy of Price Brothers.

William Gilmour worked for Price Brothers and in 1940 was working in a maintenance position in the paper mill at Riverbend. Gilly was very much of the family tradition of the Price family of working your way up the ladder from the lower ranks. He married Maimie Ida Elizabeth Fletcher from Lachute in 1938 or 1939. He had been courting her for many years but was not allowed to marry earlier due to the company policy at the time. His nieces Joan and Susan Williams were flower girls at their wedding, and remember the reception at 16 St. Denis Avenue.

Gilmour died in an industrial accident while maintaining a paper machine at the Riverbend Mill on July 9, 1940, at the age of thirty. This was two months before his son, also named William Gilmour (and usually known as Gil), was born. Ida was living in Kenogami at the time of the accident.

In those days industrial plants did not use lock-out techniques (known in French as *cadenessage*) to ensure that equipment could not accidentally be put into motion while workers were in vulnerable situations, such as when they were repairing a machine. Since that time when workers needed to maintain a piece of equipment such as a paper machine, the maintenance worker physically locks the control panel and keeps the key with him to ensure that nobody can accidentally start it up.

A beautiful stained glass window in remembrance of Gilly was commissioned and initially located in the Anglican chapel in Riverbend. Later it was moved to the Sir William Price Museum in Kenogami where it is found today at one end of the chapel facing the stained glass window made in memory of Sir William Price at the other end.

Ida worked as a teacher to support herself and Gil and was Vice-Principal at the High School of Quebec for many years. She spent the summers running a shop in Metis Beach and sent Gil to Sedburgh School near Montebello. After retirement, she went into real estate in Montreal. She died in 1990.

Gil married Gayle Lennon and had two sons, Andrew Gilmour in 1970 and Peter Llewellyn in 1972. Gil later moved to Constable, N.Y. near Cornwall, Ont., and was remarried to a woman named Lady. He died in 2019 after picking up a disease in the Philippines.

As a postlude to the tragedy of Gilmour's death, Ida and her grandsons Andrew and Peter were part of the Saguenay tour prior to the 1992 Price Family reunion in Tadoussac. While in Kenogami, Ida had an emotional meeting with the woman, a former employee of Price Brothers, who had brought her the news of Gilmour's death over fifty years before.

Micheline (Caron) 1910-1969
& George Kenilworth Craig 1902-1971

Oh song of Northern Valleys,
Played upon the winds
That sweep across the wilderness
Of tamaracks and pines,
In that sweet, wild abandon
Of a dark glade midst the trees,
Oh, let me drink the passion
Of your spirit to the lees.

There was a smile you gave me
That was native to the land
Of wide and tossing oceans
And of silver sifting sand,
It set my blood a-tingling
And I felt the call of love
While the northern stars kept twinkling
In the Heavens far above.

You may, perchance, forget me
As years flit quickly by,
Perhaps a fleeting memory
In a pale star-scattered sky.
Not so with me; forever
Will I live in that warm bliss –
The soft enduring fragrance
Of Micheline's sweet kiss.

"*Micheline on the Saguenay*" by A. G. Bailey

Not many people can claim to be the inspiration for a published poet's work, but Micheline Caron could. She is said to have been so beautiful that Canadian poet, Alfred G. Bailey, included the above in his first book of poems called *Songs of the Saguenay*. Called "Mike" by her

English friends and her family, she was also a great cook, so great that her apple and blueberry pies were legendary!

Her parents were Anita Dion and Joseph Eugène Caron who lived in Quebec City. Micheline's great-grandfather, Michel, is credited with bringing the family to Tadoussac. He worked for Price Brothers Lumber at the top of the Saguenay, and for a time was mayor of Chicoutimi. He later moved to Tadoussac, still with Price Brothers, when he was promoted to "Agent de la Couronne pour la Region de Charlevoix et le Saguenay." In this work, he had responsibilities both for the forests and the fisheries. His son, Eugene Caron, (Micheline's grandfather) was mayor of Tadoussac (1899-1927). Up until about 1960, there was a bridge over the gully on Rue des Pionniers leading up the hill toward our chapel. This was named Pont Caron, after Eugene.

In Tadoussac, the family lived in the house that is currently the chapel rectory and then moved to the Coté house around the corner that became the post office. This is the same building that later became the Gite (B & B) called *Passe-Pierre*.

Micheline was born in Tadoussac in July of 1910, but her family lived in Quebec City and she attended school at the Ursulines. It was in Quebec that she met her future husband, George.

George Craig was born in Quebec City in 1902. His father was Thomas Craig, who was the head of the Ross Rifle Company, a very prominent supplier to the Canadian Military in the first part of the century. George attended Bishop's College School in Lennoxville but finished at the Boys High School in Quebec City. His family was staunchly Presbyterian, and it was in a Presbyterian church in Quebec City that he and Micheline were wed in 1935. This suggests a certain bravery on Micheline's part. She had been brought up Roman Catholic and was told she would go to hell for marrying a Protestant!

George and Micheline's daughter, Louise, (who became known as Popsy) was born in Quebec City but then the family settled in Kenogami where George worked for H. B. Bignal Insurance. This was the company that insured the Price Brothers company, among others. They were great friends with the Prices and their son, Ian, who was born there in 1941, remembers babysitting Cynthia Price. He was also a very close friend of

Toby Price. When the children were grown up, the family moved back to Quebec City.

Both George and Micheline were very enthusiastic about fly fishing and very strict in their pursuit of that sport. Wet flies only, please, and careful adherence to local regulations and quotas. They were very active members of the Onatchiway Fish and Game Club, due north of Chicoutimi, situated on land where the Price Lumber Company was logging. They loved Tadoussac and also fished locally in the Marguerite River and Les Bergeronnes with their children.

When in Tadoussac, Micheline and George always stayed with Mary and Lex Smith who owned *Bayview Cottage* until the mid-1960s. It was a very busy place in those days, centrally located, with lots of people dropping in. They were very close friends and some summers the two couples would cruise from Quebec City to Tadoussac together on Lex's powerboat, the *Lady Mary*. Arthur Smith, who was Lex's "Uncle Art," would often drop by in the evenings from where he stayed at the nearby Boulianne Hotel (situated where L'Hotel Les Pionniers is today.) On one memorable occasion, the Craig family were all out on Uncle Art's boat, *Empress of Tadoussac*, and arrived from the Saguenay just as the CSL boat *Quebec* was entering the bay on fire. They were directed to head out into the river to see if anyone had jumped overboard but thankfully, only found a deckchair.

When the Smiths wanted to sell *Bayview*, George and Micheline's daughter and her husband (Popsy and Robert) were very tempted to buy it, but they passed on the opportunity in spite of saying that many of the family's happiest times had been spent in Tadoussac. The cottage was subsequently bought by Dennis and Sue Stairs and has remained in the Stairs family ever since.

At the age of fifty-nine, Micheline had a very sudden heart attack at her home in Quebec City. She died in her son's arms before she could even get to the hospital. After her death, George moved to Washington for a short time to stay with their daughter Popsy and her family. That worked well at first, but he missed Quebec City where he always felt more at home. He returned, but also suffered a heart attack and died in 1971, two years after he had lost Micheline.

Robert Lewis Evans 1911-1988
& Elizabeth Anne (Morewood) Evans
1922-1993

In 1911, Emily Elizabeth (Bethune) Evans, at age forty-six, gave birth to her only child, Robert Lewis Evans. Her husband, the Very Reverend (Dean) Thomas Frye Lewis Evans, was sixty-seven, father of five adult children and grandfather of two young ones.

In 1922, Caroline Annie (Rhodes) Morewood, at age forty-two, gave birth to her second child, Elizabeth Anne (Betty) Morewood. Her husband was her first cousin, Francis Edmund Morewood, who was five years her junior. They already had a son, William Harold Morewood.

In the summer of 1944, at the Coupe in Tadoussac, thirty-three-year-old Lewis asked twenty-one-year-old Betty to marry him. She said yes, and their lives came together in December of that year.

Until the Dean died in 1920, the Evans family had spent their winters in Montreal and every summer in their house in Tadoussac, which at that time was the farthest east of the Price Brothers houses and would later be sold to the Beatties. After his death, however, mother and son moved to Toronto for the winters but still got to Tadoussac each year.

Emily sent Lewis to Trinity College School – a boys' boarding school in Port Hope, Ontario. Lewis liked the school and had positive memories of it. This is remarkable because, on a personal level, these were difficult years. At the age of fourteen, he was hit by a severe case of alopecia, an autoimmune disorder whereby one's hair falls out, and over the next year or so, he lost all his hair.

Between graduating from TCS and starting at Trinity College in Toronto, Lewis was taken on a European tour by his mother. They travelled extensively and visited many specialists in an effort to reverse the effects of alopecia. It was after this tour that Lewis chose to wear a wig, a decision he frequently regretted especially in the heat of the summer.

Meanwhile, Betty, one of Col. William Rhodes's many great-grandchildren, was growing up in Doylestown, Pennsylvania. She attended the Baldwin School for girls and subsequently Bryn Mawr

Lewis & Betty aboard the Noroua

and the University of Pennsylvania. Her family would spend time in Tadoussac most summers, renting rooms in *Catelier House* (now the Maison du Tourisme). In 1936, her father designed and built a house, now called *Windward*. From then on, she never missed a summer in Tadoussac.

In 1948, Frank and Carrie Morewood sold *Windward* to Betty and Lewis for $1, and suddenly, Lewis, whose mother had died the year before, found himself with two cottages in Tadoussac. He chose to keep *Windward*, partly because it was newer, partly because it was politic, partly because of its view, but especially because he could see his boat at its buoy in the bay!

At university, Lewis had studied English, graduating in 1933, and Betty had majored in business, graduating in 1944. Lewis followed through on his plan to be a teacher and started his career in 1934 at Bishop's College School from which he retired in 1972.

Any career plans Betty had upon graduation were trumped by her summer engagement and winter wedding... and in the fullness of time, by the arrival of Anne, Lewis, Tom, and Alan. She was of the generation when women were mothers and homemakers, and to these functions, Betty added the role of steadfast supporter of all that her husband did, and BCS benefitted from her unpaid and often unknown contribution. For the first eighteen years of their marriage, Lewis was a Housemaster. Betty knew all the boys and welcomed them into her home as a matter of course. Every teacher new to BCS was invited to Sunday dinner, and she frequently found herself hosting parties for faculty and friends. She has been called a world-class knitter and a world-class worrier (especially about her children no matter how old they were).

Meanwhile, Lewis was completely immersed in the life of the school – teaching, coaching, directing plays, and running his residences. He was one of the pioneers of ski racing in the Eastern Townships and spent many hours freezing at the bottom of a hill, clipboard in one hand and stopwatch in the other. He was an example of service and character. When he died, one Old Boy remembered him as "an oasis of calm in an otherwise harsh and demanding school." Indeed, he was.

But his contributions went beyond BCS. From the mid-50s until his retirement in 1972, he spearheaded the Lennoxville Players, directing many plays from British farces to Broadway musicals. This was a group of amateur "actors" from all levels of the community who were, like their leader, looking for an enjoyable night out ... and all proceeds to go to a local charity.

In 1972, Betty and Lewis retired to Brockville, Ontario. Here, they joined Tadoussac friends, Ray and Coosie Price and Jean and Guy Smith. From there, they travelled to Tadoussac – for many years by boat.

An accomplished sailor, Lewis knew every cove and anchorage on the Saguenay, learned from his own experience, but even more, from local captains whom he respected and adored, and, it would seem, who held him in equal esteem. Over the years, his passion for boats gave way to his passion for fishing. There were many overnight trips up the Saguenay, often to the Marguerite, to fish the falling tide, then the rising, then up early to start again. One can still see him standing in hip-waders off the point above the crib, rod in hand, pipe upside down against the drizzle, as dawn was lighting the sky.

Betty and Lewis were practising Christians, and while their church in Lennoxville tended to be the BCS Chapel, the one that they were most committed to was the Tadoussac Protestant Chapel. Betty's great-grandfather had been instrumental in its creation, and Lewis's father, the Dean, had, for decades, been the summer priest. In 1972, Betty undertook to organise several summer residents to needlepoint the altar kneeler cushions with images of local wildflowers designed by her close friend Barbara Campbell, and for many years, Lewis served as the secretary on the church committee executive.

And then there was golf, which Betty loved, and Lewis tolerated, and bridge, which... Betty loved, and Lewis tolerated.

For all their lives, home was where the family was, but Tadoussac was where the family was at home. Their love for Tadoussac is best articulated in Lewis's memoir, *Tides of Tadoussac*, which included the Rudyard Kipling quotation:

"God gave all men all earth to love
But since our hearts are small,
Ordained for each one place should prove
Beloved overall."

His fascination with the history of the place was likewise revealed in his fictional book *Privateers and Traders*.

Theirs was a great love, a love of each other, a love of family and friends, a love of people and community, and a love of place, and that love of place, of that place, of Tadoussac, has been inherited by each of their four children and by each of their families.

H. Edward C. Price 1916-1995 &
Mary Winifred (Hampson) 1917-1977

Henry Edward Clifford (Teddy) Price was born in Quebec City in 1916, the eighth child and third son of Harry Price and Muriel Gilmour. He grew up in Quebec among his family at 2 and 18 rue Saint-Denis in old Quebec near the Citadel. He spent his summers in Tadoussac where he had many friends including Jim and Jean Alexander and met his wife Mary Hampson in the mid-1930s. From 1929 to 1931 he attended Trinity College School in Port Hope but was withdrawn when he became homesick. When he wanted to go back later, the family could no longer afford it having lost money in the depression. He graduated in 1935 from the High School of Quebec, and attended the Royal Military College in Kingston, just as many of his relatives did before him.

Mary Winifred Hampson was born in Montreal in 1917, to Edward Greville Hampson and Helen Winifred Stanway. She grew up in Montreal with her younger sister Barbara Isabel, and brother, John Greville. They lived initially on Bishop Street and later moved to 1501 MacGregor Street at the corner of Simpson. (MacGregor Street had its name changed to Avenue Docteur Penfield long after the Hampsons sold their house.) As well as their house in Montreal, the Hampsons acquired a farm near Ste. Therese where they spent their weekends.

Mary attended the Study School in Montreal and was a boarder at Elmwood School in Ottawa from which she graduated in 1935. She later attended finishing schools in Germany and England. She was not allowed to attend university by her father who did not believe girls should attend university. Instead, she used to audit the courses for her friends at McGill so they would be marked as present at their lectures when they were absent. For the rest of her life, she always enjoyed reading books to make up for her lack of a university career but made sure her daughters were properly educated.

The Hampsons spent many summers in Murray Bay and Cap a l'Aigle. Sometime in the mid-1930s the Hampsons came to Tadoussac by boat and stayed at the Hotel Tadoussac. There Mary encountered many friends, including her future husband Ted Price, as well as Jim

Alexander who would marry her sister Barbara.

At the start of World War II in 1939, Ted joined the Canadian Army and was commissioned as a Lieutenant in the Permanent Force and went overseas with the Royal Canadian Regiment. Prior to his departure he and Mary were married on a week's notice on November 18, 1939, at St. George's Church in Montreal.

Mary followed Ted overseas to Surrey, England where they set up house in *Yew Tree Cottage* in Lower Kingswood near Reigate, Surrey and their four children were born: Greville in February 1941, twins Tim and Ginny in January 1943, and Sally in September 1944.

In 1942 Ted was transferred to the headquarters of the 1st Canadian Infantry Division in England and served in the Allied invasion of Sicily and Italy. After attending the British Army Staff College in 1944 he was posted to the 2nd Canadian Infantry Division in the United Kingdom and North-West Europe until the end of the war.

In August 1945, the family returned to Canada where they received a tremendous welcome coming off the boat in Tadoussac meeting parents, siblings, cousins, and friends they had not seen in many years. Ted remained in the Army after the war serving in a variety of military positions. His many postings included Kingston, Ottawa, Vancouver, and England. Then he was back to Canada in Petawawa before going to Germany, then Victoria, Newfoundland, and even Tanzania before his final posting in Washington. He retired from the Canadian army in 1970 with the rank of Colonel.

The family went with Ted on all these moves, which came regularly every two to three years. It was up to Mary to find a home (if a PMQ was not allotted by the army), find schools for the children, make new friends, or find out if they knew some of the military families from previous postings, and get to know some friends in the new location. In 1946 they purchased a house at 118 Lisgar Road, Rockcliffe as a pied de terre, whenever they were in Ottawa, and as a place to retire, which they did in 1970.

Mary took advantage of the frequent moves to take the family with or without Ted on trips around British Columbia, England, or Europe. When the family were older, they would bring their spouses and later

Jimmy & Bar Alexander with baby Michael
Mary & Teddy Price with baby Greville

grandchildren to the postings in Tanzania for the game parks, and Washington. The trips were always well-planned.

Ted remained active in many charitable activities, particularly the Order of St. Lazarus as its Secretary General for several years. He was active as a golfer at the Royal Ottawa Golf Club and was a member of the Rideau Club where he served a term as Secretary. He also enjoyed tennis, squash and skiing. He was a keen fisherman belonging to several fishing clubs, particularly the Magnassippi Angling Club near Deux Rivieres, Ontario.

In 1956, Mary bought Ted's family's summer house, the *Harry Price House*, in Tadoussac from her brother-in-law Jimmy, so she was able to spend most summers in Tadoussac. Every summer after Ted retired, she was able to get to Tad from most places in North America, except the west coast. While in Tadoussac she enjoyed the picnics, played bridge with many friends, read books, swam in the lake and entertained friends and relatives. She introduced her many friends they had met during the army days to the Saguenay and their Tadoussac friends.

During his retirement leave at the start of 1970, Ted and Mary embarked on a long-planned round-the-world tour to see their many friends in many places.

After retirement, Mary and Ted lived in their house in Ottawa and watched their four children all get married between 1966 and 1972 and eventually grandchildren arrived. They enjoyed visiting Ginny and Randy in Newfoundland, Sally and Ross in Somerset, England, Tim and Frances in Montreal and Antigua, and Greville and Kerry who remained in Ottawa. Mary got sick in the fall of 1976 and died of pancreatic cancer in April 1977, three months before her 60th birthday.

Ted remained strongly committed to the Price family corresponding with many relatives in various parts of the world in the 1970s and 1980s, building up voluminous files. He developed the initial family tree in 1974. He supported the start of the reunions in 1987 and gave the address to the 1992 Tadoussac reunion at the Tadoussac Protestant Chapel.

In 1971, Ted joined the Standards Council of Canada on its formation, serving as its Director of Administration and Secretary General until his second retirement in July 1981. After Mary died, Ted married Martha "Marty" Eberts, who was also recently widowed. She had been the wife of Chris Eberts, the brother of Bea Eberts who was married to Ted's cousin Charlie Price. They lived in Ottawa and were very supportive of their families.

Marty developed dementia and in 1990 had to be admitted to a home, which was stressful for Ted. He developed prostate cancer and died on November 16, 1995, in Ottawa with his funeral being held two days later on the date of his original wedding anniversary. At his memorial service a few days later, the eulogy was given by his godson Tony Price.

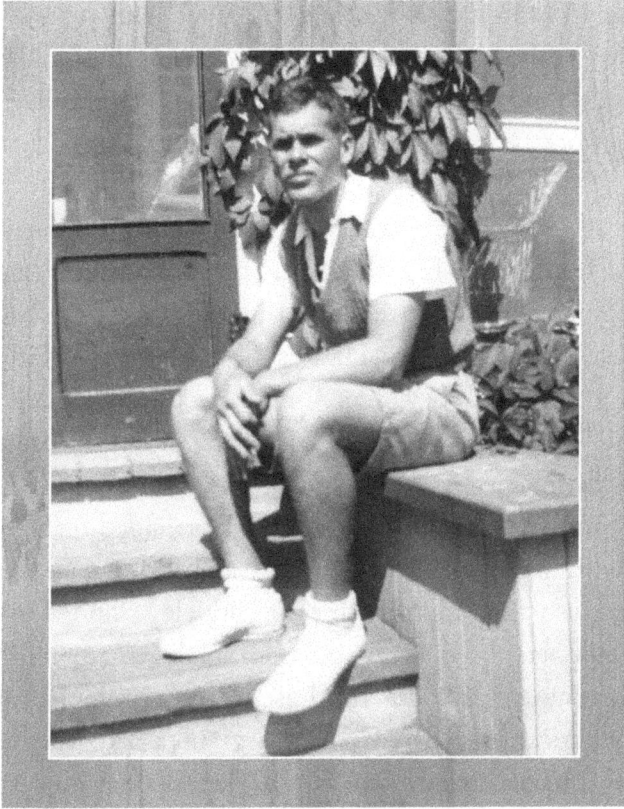

Jimmy Alexander at Brynhyfryd

James Okeden Alexander 1918-1941

Born in 1918, at Caterham, Surrey in England while his father was fighting in the trenches during World War I, and his mother was in England. Jimmy was the eldest grandchild of Bishop Lennox W. Williams and Annie (Nan) Rhodes. At age twelve he went to Bishop's College School. He ran in five cross-country races, became a marksman, wrote poetry and had Lewis Evans as his English teacher. After graduating in 1935, he won the Greenshields Scholarship to McGill University, which he declined because he entered Royal Military College in Kingston. He graduated from RMC in 1939 with the first prize in mechanical and electrical engineering and the Harris-Bigelow trophy for the best combination of athletic and academic ability.

Jimmy's summers were spent in Tadoussac at his grandparent's house, *Brynhyfryd*, with his mother, his sister Jean Aylan-Parker, and cousins Nan (Wallace) Leggat and her brother Jackie Wallace. Among his many childhood friends were Ted and Evan Price, Billy Morewood, Betty (Morewood) Evans, Phoebe (Evans) Skutezky and Ainslie (Evans) Stephen.

In July of 1936, Jimmy and his friend Teddy Price stood on the wharf as the CSL steamship pulled in. Soon a roadster bumped its way up the gangplank onto the dock and in the back were two beautiful young sisters, Bar and Mary Hampson, aged sixteen and seventeen. Teddy said to Jimmy; "That one's mine!" and Jimmy replied, "the other one's for me!" Four years later as World War II began, Jimmy married Bar and Teddy married Mary.

When Jimmy graduated from RMC, he decided on a career in the air force. He trained with the RCAF at Camp Borden and Trenton and was awarded his wings and the Sir John Siddeley trophy for the highest marks and qualities as a pilot. As the then small Canadian force had few career opportunities for flying, he chose a career in the Royal Air Force and on graduation from RMC he was granted a regular commission in the RAF. The dark clouds of World War II were approaching, and the summer of 1938 was the last time the family was all together in Tadoussac. His father, Major General Ronald Alexander would assume Pacific Command as the war began. His mother, Gertrude Williams, would also move to Victoria B.C. with his brother Ronnie (aged seven). His sister, Jean, would marry John Aylan-Parker and go overseas to the war in early 1940.

Jimmy sailed to England in March 1940 to join the RAF for a career in the permanent force. Bar followed soon after and they were married in England in early May. Jimmy went over to France with the Air Advanced Striking Force. As the German forces drove the allies back to the English Channel and France collapsed, the historic evacuation from Dunkirk and other French ports saved the retreating armies and brought them back to England to fight again. Jimmy's squadron abandoned their aircraft and he found himself on the liner *Lancastria* being evacuated with over five thousand others. The ship was bombed and quickly sank. Jimmy went overboard, was rescued but soon dove in again to save a woman's life and was later awarded the Royal Humane Society Medal for Valour.

During 1940 and 1941, Jimmy and Bar moved with his squadron wherever it was based. After a few months with his squadron in Iceland, he went to Northern Ireland. Bar was in Suffolk in December 1940 when their son Michael was born. They all settled in Belfast in January 1941, but their home was bombed while they were away at Easter. As war raged and the German Luftwaffe was bombing England's cities, they were able to get together with Ted and Mary Price (Bar's sister) and John and Jean Aylan-Parker (Jimmy's sister) who were also stationed in England. Michael, Greville Price and Ronnie Aylan-Parker were all born within months of each other. Jimmy was now flying almost daily raids over enemy territory with RAF Bomber Command Squadron 88. In the summer of 1941, as Flight Lieutenant with two crew members, he flew his Blenheim bomber from their base in Norfolk. Their targets were the factories and shipping in German-occupied Rotterdam, Holland. The Dutch were friends and allies. Jimmy's squadron flew in daylight, as low as possible over the factories, so they could bomb accurately and avoid killing the civilian population. Winston Churchill described it. "The devotion and gallantry of the attack on Rotterdam is beyond all praise. The charge of the Light Brigade at Balaclava is eclipsed in brightness by these daily deeds of fame."

On August 28, 1941, Jimmy and his crew were shot down over Rotterdam. He is buried there in Croswijck Municipal Cemetery beside the graves of his two crew. He was twenty-three years old. Today, one hundred and thirty-five graves of young fliers from Commonwealth countries who were killed over Holland from 1940-44 lie there in rows. They were all under the age of twenty-five.

In his memoirs, his father Ronald describes Jimmy's outlook on life as: "... such a happy one and he hated seeing anybody unhappy. He loved all games, flying, seeing new places, and his fellow men. His God, his faith and his religion meant a great deal to him and were very real. Poetry appealed to him. In one of his letters from RMC he wrote: 'Sometimes I think I'd like to take up poetry seriously, but it is rather a life for men of mind and not men who have physical abilities. But a poet does so much for mankind.'"

While at BCS, seven years before, Jimmy wrote a poem titled 'To Friends'. This is the final verse:

Long after friends have left us,
their memory still will last;
The memory of those happy days,
those days that now are past:
And we will not forget them,
until at last we be
With them once more united,
for all eternity.

Jimmy's short life was full. However, life goes on in his legacy: his wife, Bar (Hampson) Campbell who died in September 2008; his son Michael and wife Judy; his two grandchildren, Nan (Doyal) and Jim Alexander and five great-grandchildren. They all spend part of their summers in Tadoussac.

Llewellyn Evan Price 1919-1944

Evan was the youngest son of Henry Edward and Helen Gilmour Price. He grew up in a family of ten siblings of ages ranging over twenty years. They all spent their summers in Tadoussac at the *Harry Price House*. Evan grew up in Quebec City and attended Quebec High School. As a teenager in Tadoussac, his active young group of friends included his older brother Ted, Jimmy Alexander, Jean (Alexander) Aylan-Parker, Betty (Morewood) Evans, Phoebe (Evans) Skutezky, Ainslie (Evans) Stephen, Mary (Hampson) Price, Barbara (Hampson) Alexander, Nan (Wallace) Leggat, and Jackie Wallace.

When World War II was declared, Evan joined the Royal Canadian Airforce. He did his pilot training at Camp Borden and Trenton and went overseas in 1940. He was assigned to North Africa where he took part in the allied advance from El Alamein to Tripoli. In 1943 Flight Lieutenant Evan Price returned to Canada as a flight instructor at the RCAF Operational Training Base at Bagotville, Quebec. Six months later, in January 1944, while flying to Quebec to attend the funeral of Lt. Col. "Canon" Scott, his plane crashed near Baie St. Paul. He is buried in Mount Hermon Cemetery in Quebec.

Gertrude Anne (Wallace) Leggat 1920-1983 & Walter Creighton Leggat 1912-1992

Nan, named after her grandmother, Caroline Annie Rhodes was born in the original Rhodes house in Tadoussac in 1920, to Mary (Williams) and Jack Wallace. She was the great-granddaughter of Colonel William and Anne Catherine (Dunn) Rhodes and she and Bob spent their summers in Tadoussac in *Brynhyfryd* with her parents along with the many guests who frequented what was referred to as "The Big House".

Nan enjoyed the company of her many cousins and friends, played golf and tennis and played the church organ Sundays at the Protestant Chapel. Nan was a very proficient piano player able to play music by ear. In fact, it was Nan's musical talent that led her children into the music field, Michael a keyboard player and Robbie, a trumpeter and pianist. John was a soloist in St. Andrew's and St. Paul's boys' choir and a member of the RMC Choir. All four boys sang in the St. Andrew's and St. Paul's boys' choir in their youth.

Nan spent her early days living in Grand-Mère where her father worked for the Laurentide Pulp and Paper Company. She had two younger brothers, John (Jackie) Williams and Michael Sydney.

The Wallace family moved to Westmount Quebec where Nan attended Roslyn School, Miss Edgars and Miss Cramps Private School, and went on to study nursing at the Montreal General Hospital. During the Second World War, Nan was a Lieutenant and Nursing Sister posted to the Canadian Military Hospital in London, England. Upon arrival back in Montreal, Nan took on the role of corporate nurse for Molson Breweries.

Bob was born in Montreal to Eleanor and Colonel William Leggat in 1912. Siblings included Margaret Jane (MacInnes), William Hamilton (Bob's twin brother), Peter Strathern and Eleanor (Cross). They lived at 3433 Stanley Street in Montreal. The Leggat summer residence in those days was in Knowlton, Quebec on a large property overlooking Brome Lake. It was during the time spent in Knowlton that Bob became very proficient at golf, tennis, and sailing. These talents made it easy for him to enjoy the Tadoussac community lifestyle.

Nan & Bob Leggat

Bob was educated at St. Alban's School in Brockville. He entered the Royal Military College in 1929, studied military engineering, and graduated in 1933. From there he enrolled in the McGill University Law School. Prior to World War II, he joined the firm of Foster, Place, Hackett, Mulvens, Hackett and Foster in Montreal.

In 1939, he headed overseas in advance of the First Canadian Division as a Captain in the Royal Canadian Artillery. Bob was engaged in action in North Africa, Italy, Belgium, the Netherlands, and Germany and returned to Canada in 1945 as a Brigadier having been awarded the Distinguished Service Order for bravery. He commanded the Canadian Army's artillery brigade in Europe, the largest concentration of artillery in the history of the Canadian Army. Following his arrival back in Canada, Bob returned to his law practice, becoming the senior and managing partner of Leggat, Colby, Rioux, Demers, & Swift in 1969. He maintained his association with the Montreal Artillery by supporting their social activities.

In 1947, Nan and Bob were married at St. Matthias Church. The next few years would have been very busy for the couple with the birth of four boys: Robert Wallace in 1948, Lennox John in 1949, Michael Creighton in 1952, and William Walter in 1956.

With the family expanding, and after living in an apartment, a duplex at 12 Parkside Place on Cote-des-Neiges, they moved into 647 Grosvenor Avenue in 1957 where they lived until 1979. Along with raising four boys, Nan was very active in volunteering roles at the Montreal General Hospital, and at the Church of St. Andrew and St. Paul.

In addition to practising law, Bob was the president of The Canadian Corps of Commissionaires and the Saint Andrew's Society. He was the honorary solicitor for The Last Post Fund and a long-time member and trustee of the Church of St. Andrew and St. Paul.

The family's summers in Tadoussac were most definitely a high point in their lives. In fact, their children, grandchildren, and great-grandchildren continue to return every summer. One summer, Nan and Bob bought a retired lobster fishing boat from Gordon Smith and renamed it *GAL* after Nan, (Gertrude Anne Leggat). Many picnics up the Saguenay ensued in all types of weather along with overnight trips to the mouth of the Marguerite River, or St. Etienne which were out of reach for day trips on a boat that reached a maximum speed of seven knots. Bob was unable to spend the whole of the summer in Tadoussac due to work commitments and Nan took over the running of the GAL in his absence. She gained the title of "Tugboat Annie" after driving the boat up the Saguenay River when a humpback whale surfaced next to the boat close enough to be touched by those onboard.

The summer routine at *Brynhyfryd* was very regimented to accommodate the many guests who passed through. Breakfast at 08:00, Lunch at 13:00 and Supper at 19:00 summoned by a school bell ensuring everyone met together for formal meals and jovial chatter. During the time Bishop Williams, Nan's grandfather, was alive, breakfasts were preceded by morning prayers with everyone gathered in the living room. It was this order that helped the three older generations survive living with the Leggat family of four rambunctious little boys.

Nan became ill with breast cancer in 1971 and as a result, in 1972 the couple decided they would not take on ownership of the big house in Tadoussac from Mary and Jack. Instead, their love of boating led them to purchase a boat in Montreal which they kept at the Iroquois Yacht Club on Lake St. Louis. It was used as a summer cottage on weekends, and during Bob's holidays, they would go on long boat trips between Ontario and Quebec and once into Lake Champlain. The Rideau system was one of their favourite voyages.

Nan and Bob moved to Knowlton in 1979 where they spent the rest of their days at 72 St. Paul's Road. Nan passed away in 1983, after surviving twelve years of breast cancer. This was remarkable back then given the prognosis of fewer than four years. Bob suffered a stroke in 1982 but continued to live at home until his death in 1992.

Nan and Bob had an exceptionally loving relationship. They were a couple who attracted many people because of their friendly, welcoming nature and great sense of humour. Their parties were lively, usually ending up with Nan at the piano, and Bob drumming on a cake tin leading the singing of old songs sung to help soldiers endure the stress of war.

Summers at Tadoussac formed a very special family bond for the Leggat family fostering relationships between distant cousins and many close friends. Nan, as a "local" was naturally embraced by the community and Bob was welcomed with open arms when introduced by Nan, whom he continually referred to as his "Dear One".

John (Jackie) Williams Wallace 1922-1982 & Margaret (Marg) Faye (Hawkings) 1921-2009

Jackie was born in Grand-Mère, Quebec to John Reginald Wallace (1892-1975) and Violet Mary Williams (1890-1989). His older sister Gertrude Anne (Nan) (1920) was born in Tadoussac, Quebec, and his younger brother Michael Sydney (1927) was also born in Grand-Mère. The family moved to Montreal in 1931 and lived at 550 Claremont Avenue, 624 Murray Hill Road then in 1938 moved to 15 Grenville Avenue.

Jackie attended Westmount High School and after graduation entered the Royal Military College in Kingston, Ontario from 1940 -1942. His class was the last class at RMC before the college closed for the war years. While at the school, Jackie was an accomplished athlete known for his gymnastic abilities. He was also one of two cadets capable enough in seamanship that he was assigned one of the two largest

Jack & Marg aboard the Bonne Chance in 1961

sailboats in the school's fleet (about 24 feet) and was allowed to take it out when he had free time. He graduated as one of the top cadets in his class and upon graduation went on to serve as a Lieutenant in the Canadian Army in Italy. He returned from Italy injured and spent time in the Royal Victoria Hospital in Montreal where he met his future wife, Margaret Faye Hawkings through his sister Nan. Both Nan and Marg were nurses in the same hospital.

Marg was born in Kenogami, Quebec to Clarence Stanley Victor Hawkings (1894-1960) and Queenie Laura Norton (1898-1988). Clarence worked as a chemist at the Price Brothers pulp and paper mill in Jonquiere, Quebec and went on to become Mill Manager until his retirement. Her older brother, Robert (Bob) Clarence Hawkings, was born in 1919 in Ottawa, Ontario, her younger sister, Dorothy Ward Hawkings, was born in 1922, in Toronto, Ontario and her younger brother, William (Bill) Edgar Hawkings, was born in 1931, in Kenogami.

Marg was adventurous. She once travelled to Boston on the back of a motorcycle to see a young man! In addition, she left Kenogami at a very young age to study at McMaster University in Hamilton, Ontario but decided to pursue nursing. She returned to Quebec and graduated from the Royal Victoria Hospital.

Jackie and Marg were married in Kenogami in 1946. They moved to Montreal where Jackie received his B.Sc. degree in Mechanical Engineering from McGill University in 1949. They continued to live on Grenville Avenue with Jackie's parents and their first-born child, Deborah Anne, was born in 1947. After graduation, the family moved to Hamilton, Ontario and lived at 250 East 16th Street. A second daughter, Elizabeth Jean, was born in 1950. The family moved to Burlington, Ontario, 4418 Spruce Avenue, in 1958.

Jackie joined the Canadian Westinghouse Company as a metallurgist and was a foundry engineer from 1950-59. He went on to become superintendent of the foundry from 1959-1962. In 1962 he became Vice-President and General Manager of George F. Pettinos (Canada) Ltd., which was a Canadian manufacturer and distributor of foundry supplies and industrial minerals. He was also a former National Director of the American Foundrymen's Society.

Jackie and Marg and their two daughters spent many summers in Tadoussac with Jackie's parents at the Wallace family summer home, *Brynhyfryd*. They were great friends with Lewis and Betty Evans, even cruising with them on their boat from Kingston, Ontario all the way to Tadoussac in 1967 with a stop at the Montreal Expo World's Fair on the way. When Lewis and Betty's daughter Anne married and settled near Burlington, Jack and Marg had her and her husband Ian in for dinner frequently and even helped them in the process of buying their first house.

They also spent time in the summer in Kenogami with Marg's family where they fished and enjoyed the Lac St. Jean area. Jackie and Marg bought a sailboat in the mid-1970s which they kept at the yacht club in Oakville. Many a pleasant day and evening was spent on the *Beluga* on Lake Ontario. Marg had a variety of interests and kept busy with many volunteer activities. In particular, she volunteered for several years with the Girl Guides of Canada. She was an excellent seamstress, an amazing cook and loved to entertain. She travelled extensively, even into her late 80s and took every opportunity to attend live theatre. She was an avid fan of professional golf, football and hockey, even cheering for the Montreal Canadians when all their friends were true Toronto fans. Marg loved life, had a great sense of humour and laughed easily.

Jackie had many interests including gardening (especially roses), woodworking, and photography (who could forget the always-present movie camera at all events) but at the top of his list, he was a strong believer in family. He would travel anywhere, through anything to be with family and is remembered by all as a very kind, caring, fun-loving person. Trips to Montreal and Tadoussac were punctuated with many stops to see family along the route.

He had a strong passion for sailing and was at peace on the water. He was full of life and loved entertaining friends. Truly he was a full sail in a strong wind.

Dennis W. Stairs 1923-1975 &
Susan E. (Inglis) Stairs 1923-1978

Dennis was born and grew up in Montreal. After attending Bishop's College School, he joined the Royal Navy and served on the British aircraft carrier *Indefatigable* as an airplane navigator. He started coming to Tadoussac at an early age, and in his teens went on trips to Les Escoumins and the Marguerite in nor'shore canoes with his brothers and his cousin Peter Turcot - twenty miles rowing is a long way! He was a tennis and skiing enthusiast and was on the McGill University teams for both sports. He graduated from McGill with honours in engineering and took a position with what was then the Price Brothers Company in Kenogami. He married twice having four children by his first marriage and three by his second.

Sue Inglis was born and grew up in Pittenweem, Scotland. She moved to London during the war and served in an anti-aircraft unit defending the city. She married Dennis Stairs in 1957 and together they had three children, Alan, John, and Sarah to add to Dennis's previous four, Judy, George, Felicite, and Philippa, and she treated all seven with the same mixture of poise, no-nonsense strength, and kindness.

Sue had left her home in a thriving metropolitan city to move to Kenogami, a small town a mere ninety miles from Tadoussac. She adapted well, learning to ski as well as other winter activities. She also learned French well enough to lead the Girl Guides in the Lac St-Jean region!

She came to Tadoussac soon after arriving and embarked on the full range of activities – witness her name on the Mixed-Doubles Tennis Trophy in more than one place, her embroidery creations in the church, and the Scottish-dancing parties she hosted - not to mention numerous picnics around Tadoussac on the beaches, in the hills, and along the shores in the freighter-canoe *Seven Steps*. She tirelessly nursed Dennis when he took ill, enabling him to spend the last few years of his life in the relative peace and comfort of his own homes in Montreal and in Tadoussac.

Dennis passed on to all his children, with varying degrees of success, his love of the outdoors whether hiking, cross-country skiing, chopping wood, or fishing. He passed along to them his love of small boats, be they canoes, rowboats, motorboats, or even how to use a freighter canoe as a sailboat! And of course, he led by example in tennis and skiing. Perhaps most of all he tried to teach his children to be honest, fair, hard-working, and family-oriented people. Many a time they were cajoled into doing unpleasant tasks with the words "you're not going to let your poor father do everything are you?"

Dennis and Sue's children and the entire Tadoussac community remember them as good parents.

Mathieu Kane d. 1945

Mathieu Kane, known as "Bobbins", was the only child of Mathieu Charles Ralph Alonso Kane. Sadly, Bobbins was killed in Belgium on January 6th, 1945, while serving at an air observation post in Holland where he was attached to the Royal Canadian Artillery. Little else is known about his life here in Canada.

His father, Mathieu, worked for the Price Brothers Company and was a great friend of Coosie Price. Upon his death, much of his estate was left to Coosie, but rather than simply accept it, Coosie used the money to set up what became known as the Mathieu Ralph Kane Foundation. The foundation was designed to distribute the estate in a way that contributed to causes related to the church, education, medicine, conservation, environment and heritage largely in the Saguenay and Quebec City regions.

The organ in the chapel was paid for by the Kane Foundation to honour Mathieu's son Bobbins.

The Right Reverend Allen Goodings
1925-1992

In 1964, the Reverend Allen Goodings enquired at the Diocesan office in Montreal about the possibility of becoming a locum over the summer months. Advised that nothing was vacant, the secretary put forward his name should a placement become available. Early in July, he unexpectedly received a phone call asking if he would be interested in presiding over services at the Tadoussac Protestant Chapel the following month. Neither he nor his wife Joanne knew much about where they were headed but a few weeks later a trunk was loaded onto a CSL steamship, and with their car packed to the roof, the family set off on an adventure that was to be repeated almost yearly for the next two decades.

Allen Goodings was born in 1925, in Barrow-in-Furness, Lancashire, England. The second of three children, he was born into a shipbuilding family. His father Thomas was in the employ of His Majesty's Colonial Service in the protectorate of Nigeria overseeing the building of steamships, and Allen followed his older brother Goff into an apprenticeship at Vickers Armstrong's shipyard in Barrow. He furthered his craft at Barrow Technical College and though he would rather be playing sports than studying, he eventually graduated as an engineering draughtsman. Allen, a passionate sportsman, was selected to play rugby for Lancashire County at Wembley stadium in London. He had the prospect of a professional rugby career but chose to follow another path.

On March 29, 1952, Allen sailed from Liverpool to begin a position with Vickers Armstrong's Shipbuilders, Ltd. in Montreal. Being a gregarious man, he set about building a life in Canada but gradually came to realize that he was being pulled towards another vocation. In the fall of 1952, he began a Bachelor of Arts degree at Sir George Williams College. The following year, he also began a Bachelor of Divinity at the Diocesan Theological College of McGill University. In the spring of 1959, he graduated with a degree from both universities and was ordained in December. He married Joanne Talbot of Grand Valley, Ontario, on October 26th of that same year. They went on to have two children, Suzanne and Thomas, shortly thereafter.

Over the next ten years, Allen served three parishes in the Anglican Diocese of Montreal and was chaplain to the Grenadier Guards from 1966 to 1969. His love of rugby was never far behind, and he and a group of players from the Westmount club played for Canada in the annual Bermuda Rugby Week. He was later a member of the Montreal Barbarians Rugger Club.

In the fall of 1969, he became Dean of the Cathedral of the Holy Trinity, Quebec City. On October 31, 1977, Allen was installed as the 10th Bishop of the Diocese of Quebec and served until he resigned his See in 1991. He and his wife Joanne retired to the Ottawa area the same year, where he became Assistant Bishop of Ottawa and served until his death in 1992. Tadoussac became Allen's spiritual home, a place where he made lifelong friends and lasting memories. An avid fell walker in his youth, he loved nothing more than to set off on a long ramble. He spent many happy afternoons on the tennis court and loved family picnics on Pointe Rouge communing with belugas and basking on the rocks. Allen requested that his ashes be scattered on the Saguenay River. This was done on a foggy morning in May 1992, as a whale surfaced to accompany the sailboat.

Pierre Tremblay 1926-1991

Pierre Tremblay est né à Tadoussac en 1926. Il était le quatrième d'une fratrie de cinq enfants. Sa mère Blanche Gauthier avait acquis la Maison Tremblay en héritage de sa mère Sarah Jourdain. Blanche Gauthier a épousé Armand Tremblay. Pierre a vécu toute sa vie à Tadoussac. Dès son adolescence il a commencé à travailler pour M. Hector Gauthier qui était à l'époque le « Caretaker» des cottages des estivants anglophones. Durant ses années à l'emploi de M. Gauthier, Pierre Tremblay a occupé pendant plusieurs années le poste de «Maître du quai» de la baie de Tadoussac. C'est vers l'année 1973 que Pierre Tremblay a succédé à M. Hector Gauthier pour devenir le nouveau «Caretaker» des cottages. Pierre Tremblay s'est marié en 1966 avec Thérèse Ouellet. La Maison Tremblay a été, grâce à eux, pendant des décennies, un lieu de vacances et de retrouvailles pour tous les membres de la famille Tremblay. Ils n'ont pas eu d'enfants. Par contre, ils ont toujours accordé leur hospitalité aux enfants de ses frères et plus particulièrement à ceux de son frère Maurice, capitaine sur les traversiers entre Tadoussac et Baie Ste-Catherine. Ce dernier était un artiste dans l'âme avec des talents de sculpteur et d'ébéniste. On lui doit quelques sculptures toujours en place à l'église Ste-Croix. Maurice est décédé subitement en 1975. Pierre Tremblay adorait les chiens. Quelques fois c'était deux chiens qui l'accompagnaient lors de ses visites aux cottages. Avec son épouse Thérèse, ils prenaient grand soin de la Maison Tremblay et du jardin fleuri tout autour de la maison. Pierre Tremblay a également agi pendant plusieurs années comme sacristain à la Chapelle Protestante. Il a également siégé comme marguiller pour la Fabrique Ste-Croix de Tadoussac et il a réalisé pour l'église de nombreux arrangements décoratifs lors des fêtes dominicales. Pierre Tremblay possédait des talents remarquables dans une foule de domaines. Des talents bien souvent innés mais qui ont su se perfectionner au fil de son expérience de travail. Il était un ébéniste, un charpentier et un réparateur de tous les types de problèmes que pouvaient exister dans une maison. Il fournissait en bois de chauffage les cottages des estivants, les ouvrait au printemps et les fermait à l'automne. Il les entretenait et les réparait selon les désirs de leurs propriétaires. Il était dévoué et apprécié de tous. Il a même construit la maison sise au 3 de la rue des Petites Franciscaines. Après avoir rempli des obligations le dimanche, tant à la Chapelle Protestante qu'à l'églises Ste-Croix, Pierre Tremblay aimait se reposer sur la galerie de la Maison Tremblay. Il répondait avec enthousiasme aux salutations des passants sur la rue Bord-de-l'Eau. Pierre avait un excellent sens de l'humour. Il aimait les bonnes discussions agrémentées d'un petit gin!Pierre Tremblay est décédé alors qu'il était encore jeune à l'âge de soixante-cinq ans en 1991. Il a créé un grand vide dans la vie de tous ses neveux et nièces de la famille Tremblay, dont Louis et Tina qui habitent à Tadoussac. Son épouse Thérèse l'a rejoint en 2019.

G. Douglas McCarter 1935-1985

Doug was born to Mrs. G.A. (Edna Thakray) McCarter and Brigadier General G.A. McCarter in 1935, in Ottawa, Ontario upon the return of the family from England in 1933. Doug's older sister Sallie (Sara Jane) was born in Frimley, England while their father "Nick" was in a course at the Staff College in Camberley.

Doug enjoyed a happy childhood attending the Rockliffe Park Public School and quickly became the man of the house while his father was involved in the war effort. At the age of eleven, Doug accompanied his parents to Victoria, B.C. where his father Nick retired due to ailing health. Doug finished his schooling there at Glenlyon School and University School. In 1952 he enrolled in the Royal Military College in Kingston, Ontario following in his father's footsteps. Upon graduating from RMC in 1956, Doug attended McGill University to complete his engineering degree. Doug spent the following summer in Chilliwack, B.C.

It was during this period at McGill that he met his future wife, Pam Smith, who was studying to be a nurse at the Royal Victoria Hospital, also in Montreal. After proposing to Pam in Tadoussac, Pam and Doug were married in 1958, at the Cathedral in Quebec City. Doug arranged for a full honour guard, all in RMC uniforms.

In the end, Doug chose not to pursue a military career like his father. He first accepted a position with Bell Telephone in Ottawa causing the two to move there. In 1960, their first child, (Robert Douglas) was born.

Sadly, in 1961 Doug's father died suddenly. A few weeks later their second son (William Arnold) was born. Finally, twins (Susan Elizabeth and Michael Guy) were born in 1963.

Shortly thereafter, Doug's job took the family to Montreal where they found a home in Beaconsfield. In 1968 the family once again moved to Scarsdale, New York where Doug worked for a Canadian investment firm in Manhattan. Living in the suburbs, Doug became deeply involved in work and family. He coached soccer, was a Boy Scout leader, and taught Sunday School in addition to other functions at the Church of St. James the Less where at one time he also served as warden.

Eventually, Doug's professional life saw him move to Mutual of America and other investment companies in the heart of Manhattan.

On the twins' twenty-second birthday in 1985, while out running in preparation for one of many marathons he would run, Doug suffered a massive heart attack and died at home that day. He was a devoted husband and father.

Meeting the boat 1920s

Memorials By Family

Below is a list of the memorials, organized by family. These families came to Tadoussac in the 1800s and some have descendants in the seventh and eight generations who are still here.

Price

Henry Ferrier Price	1833-1898
Sir William Price &	1867-1924
Amelia Blanche (Smith)	1863-1947
(Also in Smith list)	
Henry Edward Price &	1869-1954
Helen Muriel Gilmour	1879-1952
Frederick Courtenay Price	1877-1898
Llewellyn Price	1878-1899
Arthur Clifford Price &	1900-1982
Ethel Murray (Scott)	1899-1987
Willa (Price) Glassco	1902-1991
Helen Florence Price	1902-1981
Constance Isobel (Price) Smith	1908-1944
(Also in Smith list)	
William Gilmour Price	1910-1940
Llewellyn Evan Price	1919-1944
H. Edward C. Price &	1916-1995
Mary Winifred (Hampson)	1917-1977

Rhodes

Colonel William Rhodes	1821-1892
Armitage Rhodes &	1848-1909
Phoebe Ida (Alleman)	1854-1893
Dorothy Gwendolyn Esther (Rhodes)	1892-1977
& Trevor Ainslie Evans	1879-1938
(Also in Evans list)	

Caroline Anne (Rhodes) &	1861-1937
Lennox Waldron Williams	1859-1958
Frank Edmund Morewood &	1886-1949
Carrie Annie (Rhodes)	1881-1973
Gertrude Isobel Morewood	1891-1977
Lily Bell Rhodes	1889-1975
Monica Rhodes	1904-1985
Violet Mary (Williams) &	1890-1989
John Reginald Wallace	1892-1975
Sydney Waldron Williams	1899-1972
James Okeden Alexander	1918-1941
Gertrude Anne (Wallace) &	1920-1983
Walter Creighton Leggat	1912-1992
Elizabeth (Morewood) &	1922-1993
Lewis Evans	1911-1988
(Also in Evans list)	
John Williams Wallace &	1922-1982
Margaret Faye (Hawkings)	1921-2009

Russell

Willis Russell &	1814-1887
Rebecca Page (Sanborn)	1807-1889
Mary Francis (Russell) Janes	1864-1915
William Edward Russell	1849-1893
Fanny Elizabeth (Pope) Russell	1856-1936
Willis Robert Russell	1887-1907
Erie Russell (Janes) &	1863-1941
George de Guerry Languedoc	1860-1924
Florence Louisa Maud (Russell) Stevenson &	1877-1940
Dr James Stevenson	1878-1957
Mabel Emily (Russell) Scott	1875-1952
Adele Languedoc	1904-1993
Grace F. Scott	1904-1993

| Anne (Stevenson) & | 1915-2008 |
| The Rev Russell Dewart | 1901-1997 |

Smith

Amelia Jane (LeMesurier)	1832-1917
Robert Harcourt Smith &	1858-1913
Mary Valliere (Gunn)	1865-1931
Lt Col Herbert Carington Smith	1866-1913
Charles Carrington Smith	1867-1952
Aileen (Dawson) Smith	1874-1959
May Dawson	1870-1967
George Carington Smith	1870-1946
Edmund H. Carington Smith	1874-1951
Arthur Carington Smith	1875-1952
Sir William Price &	1867-1924
Amelia Blanche (Smith)	1863-1947
(Also in Price list)	
Alexander Harcourt Carrington Smith &	1895-1975
Mary Isobel (Atkinson) Smith	1911-1984
Gordon Carrington Smith	1906-1974
R. Guy C. Smith	1908-2006
Jean Alexandra (McCaig) Smith	1903-1988
Constance Isobel (Price) Smith	1908-1944
(Also in Price list)	
Doris Amelia Carington (Smith) &	1902-1975
Colin John Grasset Molson	1902-1997
Colonel George Noel Carington Smith	1904-1988
Colonel Herbert Carington Smith	1906-1966
Noeline Winnifred (Smith) Palmer	1902-1986
Marion Sarah (Smith) Dobson	1907-1992
George Douglas McCarter	1935-1985

Evans

Dean Lewis Evans &	1846-1920
Marie Stewart (Bethune)	1850-1903
Emily Elizabeth (Bethune)	1866-1947
Trevor Ainslie Evans &	1879-1938
Dorothy Gwendolyn Esther (Rhodes)	1892-1977
(Also in Rhodes list)	
Cyril Lewis Evans	1882-1887
Kae Evans	1909-2001
Robert Lewis Evans &	1911-1988
Elizabeth Anne (Morewood)	1922-1993
(Also in Rhodes list)	

Piddington

Alfred Piddington	1859-1922

Webb

Marjorie (Webb) Turcot	1887-1976
Dennis Webb Stairs &	1923-1975
Susan Elisabeth (Inglis) Stairs	1923-1978

Sources

The material in this book was compiled from a variety of sources including conversations, letters, and journals, as well as published resources. Below is a list of some of the published sources that were used.

tidesoftadoussac.com

Campbell, Robert. *A history, Scotch Presbyterian Church, St. Gabriel Street, Montreal.* W. Drysdale & Co., 1887.

Beattie, Benny. *Tadoussac: The Sands of Summer.* Price-Patterson, Limited, 1994.

Dewart, Ann Stevenson. *Nose to the Window*

Dictionary of Canadian Biography, vol. 11. University of Toronto/ Université Laval, 1982.
Encyclopedia of French Cultural Heritage in North America

Rhodes, Armitage. "Army's Scrapbook." *The Rhodes Saga.* Transc. Frank Morewood. Self-published, 2003

Rhodes, Godfrey. "Godfrey's Diary, 1862-1873." *The Rhodes Saga.* Transc. Frank Morewood. Self-published, 2006

Prominent People of the Province of Quebec in Professional, Social and Business Life. Publisher, 1923

The Mitre, University of Bishop's College Volume 37 No.3 December 1929

Pedigree, The Children of the (Late) Colonel William Rhodes of Benmore, Quebec, Canada